Business-to-Business Marketing Communications

Ioannis Rizomyliotis
Kleopatra Konstantoulaki
Ioannis Kostopoulos

Business-to-Business Marketing Communications

Value and Efficiency Considerations in Recessionary Times

palgrave
macmillan

Ioannis Rizomyliotis
Brighton Business School
University of Brighton
Brighton, UK

Ioannis Kostopoulos
Leeds Beckett University
Leeds, UK

Kleopatra Konstantoulaki
Westminster Business School
University of Westminster
London, UK

ISBN 978-3-319-58782-0   ISBN 978-3-319-58783-7   (eBook)
DOI 10.1007/978-3-319-58783-7

Library of Congress Control Number: 2017943622

Cover Illustration: © nemesis2207/Fotolia.co.uk

Printed on acid-free paper

This Palgrave Macmillan imprint is published by Springer Nature
The registered company is Springer International Publishing AG
The registered company address is: Gewerbestrasse 11, 6330 Cham, Switzerland

To Ektorakos

Acknowledgements

This monograph stems from Ioannis Rizomyliotis' interest in business-to-business marketing communication. His profound and ongoing focus on this neglected research area was the main inspiration for this project and gave us the motivation to put this work together. It has been a pleasure for us to work together like we have done in the past with various projects. It was quite challenging as well, as we had to merge different approaches and ideas into one commonly accepted piece of work. But, no matter how tiring and time consuming it has been, the outcome is yet one that compensates for all of our efforts.

We want to thank all the people that have inspired us during this journey, including friends and family. We would also like to offer our sincere appreciation to all those who helped with this monograph. This long list includes all those who offered their support throughout the data collection and the analysis of results.

Thanks also go to the staff at Palgrave, to Liz Barlow, in particular, for believing in the significance of this undertaking and Lucy Kidwell, who has worked with us and facilitated avoidance of any concerns or issues in the publishing process.

Finally, we would like to dedicate this book to the one and only Ektoras Rizomyliotis, for being so patient with us despite the young of his age.

Contents

List of Figures

List of Tables

1

The Significance of Business-to-Business Marketing

Abstract This chapter serves as an introduction to the role of B2B marketing in today's business environment and stresses out its importance in the contemporary economy. In this context, the authors evaluate the role of marketing communication and refer to its growing importance in B2B area. This chapter also highlights the differences between way B2B and B2C markets and describes the way businesses operate and communicate in these markets, respectively. Finally, they delve into the particularities of B2B marketing and promotion, which they attempt to clarify with the use of examples.

Keywords Business-to-business marketing · Differences between B2B and B2C · B2B marketing significance

B2B Value, Needs and Offers

The significance of business-to-business (B2B) marketing stems from the fact that purchases by organizations account for over half the economic activity in industrialized countries, with billions of pounds of spending recorded annually by individual companies. In fact, B2B activity

© The Author(s) 2017
I. Rizomyliotis et al., *Business-to-Business Marketing Communications*,
DOI 10.1007/978-3-319-58783-7_1

is 15 times greater than that in a business-to-consumer (B2C) context (Kotler 2003). At the same time, while organizational customers in the public sector continue to have massive buying power—5 to 8% of GDP in most Organization for Economic Cooperation and Development (OECD) countries (Husted and Reinecke 2009)—it is really interesting to understand how business purchases are made, especially in recessionary times, and how businesses effectively market their goods and services to organizational customers (Grönroos 2000).

In the business-to-business (B2B) sector, marketing communications are incredibly important for not just raising brand awareness, but helping individuals to make strong value judgments. Managers have vastly appreciated the importance of marketing communications in the B2C space. Still, making products appealing to business decision-makers, however, requires a different skill set to marketing to consumers. In other words, B2B marketing communications include many unique features that define the specifics of solutions needed to accomplish promotion tasks and the use of marketing tools. On top of that, the complexity of B2B products and services may dilute the positioning of B2B brands and, thus, result in numerous complications. As a result, B2B promotion has been treated as a tricky process, which produced no immediate result; a cost that could not have a profound association with the intended benefits. As the facts stand before us, it was difficult, and occasionally still is, to dissociate B2B promotion from the perception of an unnecessary marketing activity. It was taken up not as an end but as ancillary to an already established business and sales system. Small businesses, mostly but not exclusively, when surveyed, do not always get the importance of marketing communications; it is more of a cost rather than an investment for them. Over the last five decades, marketers have made great effort to establish a link between promotion (advertising mostly) and business results and provide a better understanding of value through advertising effectiveness (McBride 2007). For this, quantitative techniques and metrics have been introduced, in order to prevent promotional activities drop as the sole remedy in times of recession (Kaplan and Norton 1996).

While B2B purchases are by default high in risk and cost, the need for well-structured campaigns and accurate information provision is evident for B2B firms. Hence, communication can be the most important aspect when marketing a B2B business. Still, justifying marketing communication expenses can be difficult. This is especially true for companies that have been struggling in recent years. The worst part of the financial crisis was back in 2008 and so a distant memory for most people. However, since then, businesses have entered a double dip recession, and while we are supposedly coming out of that now, the truth is that the markets are still under a lot of pressure. Europe is unstable, with the Brexit, the potential collapse of Deutsche Bank, and other struggles all weighing on the economy of what should really be one of the markets' biggest players. Given that uncertainty, it should come as no surprise that budgets for marketing communications are stretched even in the biggest companies. Put simply, many business owners are reluctant to invest in marketing communication because it is hard to justify the expense of marketing; developing a communication strategy when there are so many other pressures on the business seems excessive. With a clearly identified sales funnel, it is easy to determine a customer value or to talk call conversion rate. With marketing communication, the effort is more enduring, and it is harder to make a clear judgment. Budgets are tight, and the first things that are usually sacrificed when a company is under budget pressure are the things that do not produce a clear and obvious revenue stream. This means that "soft things" like communication and especially long-term marketing communication activities, e.g., press relations (Christopher et al. 1991; Ballantyne 1994), will take a hit before sales, order processing and order fulfillment, or other money makers. Spending money on something that does not offer tangible returns is a hard sell—but marketing communication can be inexpensive, and it is an investment that will give businesses a real asset.

There was a time when business owners could get away with believing in the idea that if "you build it, they will come." That used to be true. New sectors were always emerging, new ideas could develop quickly, and there were plenty of untested industries and niches for people to conquer. Now, most niches are highly competitive, and this means that businesses need to offer more than just a solution to a problem in order to remain competitive (Badaracco 1991). At the same time, it is imperative for B2B marketers to find the most efficient, effective and well-justified marketing mix propositions (Varey 2001), not only to provide support against competition but also to remain in line with the recession restrictions.

The demand for the industrial market is mostly determined by the trends in the end user market. The B2B marketplace includes primary and secondary markets such as engineering, tertiary service markets and quaternary markets that are knowledge-based. Each one of these is associated with different needs. Manufacturing markets need to show high-quality products, rapid delivery and good service. The service markets need to be consistent, precise and responsive. Knowledge markets need innovation and thought leadership. The money paid by end users cover the whole value chain. Consequently, B2B marketing communication should be notably ahead of other activities in sense of the practical application of a number of new trends, innovative approaches and in breakthrough developments. In particular, B2B marketing communication efforts are concentrated on the task of increasing the gap between the perceived customer value of a product and the manufacturing costs, that is on the creation and use in marketing of the value model, including creation and increase of the business value (Lee and Park 2007). Also, B2B marketers aim at the development of mutually beneficial partnerships between suppliers, customers and other stakeholders (Jackson 1985; Quinn 1990).

Similarly, in B2B markets, the number of buyers is limited but they mostly have a professional approach to the choice of products and suppliers. Perception of purchased goods and services is based on rational considerations and not on emotions to a greater extent. Consequently, it is easier for both buyers and suppliers to understand what is really valuable for them. Respectively, if a company is not providing a unique correlation between the value of product offerings and costs, it is difficult to establish a successful and mutually beneficial long-term partnership with customers and, in turn, achieve high profitability of own business and other partners in the value chain (McDonald 1997; Rust 2000). Accordingly, while it is difficult to ensure the growth of the business value, on the contrary, effective and long-lasting partnerships can create the preconditions for increasing the gap between value and cost; the latter is a primary goal of B2B marketing communications. Expansion of the gap, the interval between the value and costs, is, in fact, one of the biggest challenges dealt with by the marketing communication function (Shaw and McDonald 2000). This consideration forms the essentiality of B2B marketing communications' importance for any company.

According to the research (Cornelissen 2009; Ernst 2011), the significance of marketing communications for B2B companies is related to various procedures. Marketing communication is inherently a process of informing the target audience about the product and its properties. The basis for any company's success lies in the appropriate determination of the market where customers are most likely to be interested in its marketing campaign. Even the recognized market giants are focused on certain customer groups to promote their products. The marketing communication system includes a set of specialists, tools, channels and direct and indirect links to the customers (messages to them and their reactions) involved in the process of interaction between the marketing system and the external environment. Respectively, marketing communication experts of the company need to deeply understand that one can effectively convey a marketing message to the consumer using a wide variety of methods.

In recent years, the role of marketing communications in B2B has significantly enhanced along with the increase in the role of marketing. It is not enough now just to have good products and services in order to be able to improve the volume of a company's sales and its profits. Features are useful but it is benefits that will really sell in the end (Argenti et al. 2005). Customers buy benefits instead of products or services, and marketing communications should transfer such messages to he selected target market. Rather than selling products, which is what a lot of B2C companies do, it makes more sense to sell outcomes. It is outcomes that make the difference in the boardroom. The finance department does not want to pay for a new server; they want to pay for a faster Web site that would not crash during seasonal sales, and that will, therefore, improve order volumes and customer satisfaction. Marketing communications offer the chance to B2B companies to focus their offerings not just around basic needs, but also on what benefits differentiate their service from others.

At the same time, through marketing communications, businesses can effectively approach the task of finding the links in existing and emerging value chains in which they can ensure the creation of value at a lower cost. Similarly, communication can support the development of improved product offerings, pricing and distribution decisions and elaborate the specific measures to increase the gap between value and costs; essentially, they manage to employ flexible and customized activities in order to respond to customer needs. B2B marketing communication specialists need to be able to form real alternative solutions and evaluate the associated costs and benefits making both qualitative and quantitative assessments (Ewing 2009). Respectively, a firm's management can consider marketing communication costs as aimed at obtaining future benefits along with investment analysis, business planning and risk assessment. Thus, effective marketing communication empowers the B2B company not only with the opportunity to take into account the interests of its customers, but also with the prospect to live by them. Business value is determined by the size of the projected cash flows, including those caused by the implementation of certain marketing communication decisions.

Soft Skills for a Hard Industry

Marketers have traditionally separated the B2B and B2C markets and worked under the assumption that there is a big perception of the difference between those markets (Minett 2002). While B2B markets involve businesses buying from other businesses, there are many assumed differences beyond just who is buying from whom. B2B markets are made up of informed, professional buyers, and this means that the buyers care a lot about functionality and performance.

Hard sells, aggressive marketing, impulse buys and trends are not as prevalent in B2B as they are in B2C. Each B2B transaction can take a long time. There is due diligence to be concerned with. The chain is more complex than in B2C, where a good promotion will create a buyer quite quickly. There are issues of supply chains and authorizations, rollouts, research and communication. Marketing communication efforts need to be well planned, because a purchase can take months or longer to complete. Furthermore, B2B buyers face risk when they make a purchase. B2C consumers usually are not risking anything beyond the price of the product. This makes B2B buyers more cautious. However, B2B buyers tend to spend more per order, which means that every customer acquired through promotion is worth more, and that alone makes marketing communication a powerful tool.

Håkansson and Snehota (1995) suggest that B2B marketing is usually relationship driven, while B2C marketing is less formal. This is true, to an extent, but marketers on both sides can learn from each other. Today, to achieve success, B2B marketers need to communicate clearly and effectively and build a case for their company. They need to understand the needs of their prospective users and customers. At the end of the day, humans—not robots—run businesses. Those humans behave a certain way when they are consumers, so why would not they behave similarly as business buyers too? People are more likely to buy from someone they are familiar with; if businesses are not visible, then in the minds of buyers, they simply do not exist. In other words, potential and existing customers should be fully aware of the company's brand and what it stands for. On top of this, many business-to-business markets have become polarized and B2B buyers are far more price-oriented than ever before. In fact, B2B customers have become more sophisticated, having a number of knowledge-based understandings. Accordingly, they focus on specifics, they have a thorough comprehension of their industry, and they know what they need to buy, so they are not buying aspiration, or simply put a good feeling. As the above suggests, B2B marketing relies on carefully targeted and well-organized campaigns and sales managers who are trained to reinforce the messages that are initially sent out.

A part of the reason that so many people are wary of B2B marketing communication is that they tend to believe it involves expensive and complex ad campaigns, which are mostly suitable when communication with consumers.

The dichotomy between B2C and B2B comes from the way that the markets used to be, but over the last decade, the markets have changed somewhat. The truth is that while there are some clear differences between B2C consumer mentality and that of the B2B buyer, there are more similarities. B2B marketers have come to realize that the individual strategies used in the B2C world are not conflicting. Whatever the context is, businesses tend to forget that marketing communication functions as a part of the marketing framework. The kind of marketing framework that works for B2C can, with tweaks, have a huge value for B2B as well. Marketing communication is an integral part of a holistic framework, of a marketing proposition. The goals of communication are numerous, and the benefits from a successful implementation of a marketing communications' mix are several too. For the marketing strategy to be effective, the whole business needs to be on board. Pricing, product quality, customer service and delivery all need to be good to overcome concerns about the value of the offering.

The world of marketing has changed a lot in the last 10 years. Marketing communication is not all about glitzy ads and aggressive sales pitches. A large part of it is sharing clear and consistent messages and building recognition within the industry and, to a certain extent, outside of it too. Everyone has heard of IBM, even people who do not work in IT. In other words, B2B markets are slowly becoming more and more brand aware. Traditional B2B marketing tools are no longer good enough to create and deliver powerful brands. Therefore, marketing communication in a crowded and competitive marketplace needs to have a balance of important marketing elements including conventional, traditional and online elements. Developing a well-adjusted, sound and cost-effective marketing communication plan will certainly support B2B companies in their struggle to survive in competitive industries.

The challenge, for the managers that are trying to sell marketing and communication, is justifying the short-term expense and showing the value of communication (Gummesson 2002). Showing ROI for key outbound sales staff is simple, but showing ROI for a bigger, more general marketing campaign is a lot harder. Despite the use of analytics, track discount codes, survey customers and well-informed forecasts, it is never easy to persuade someone who is truly skeptical that marketing communication has value (Gummesson 2004).

The example of a global manufacturing company, hereafter designated as Company X, is an appropriate one to highlight the remarkable benefits that marketing communication offers to B2B companies. This company has eight manufacturing branches spread all over the world. It also has 22 service partners and 13 sales operations. Company X is a big company that operates worldwide, and that offers partners both concept and design skills, as well as production facilities. A big part of their selling point is enlarging business relations and cooperating closely with partners.

Company X is an innovative company. It takes pride in developing partnerships and being a one-stop shop for retail, and it aims to be a turnkey supplier. One of its key marketing messages is that it is a global supplier with local knowledge. It operates across borders, and it aims to maximize the retail performance of everyone that it works with ñ whether that is convenience retail stores, airports, health and beauty, telecoms specialists or even pharmacies.

One of the challenges that Company X faces is that in spite of it actually supplying several household names, it is a relatively unknown company, even in its home country. Almost everyone will have seen some products made by Company X, but they would not associate the ROL brand with those products. Consumers have no idea that Company X provides shelves, fixtures or retail solutions to their favorite stores. Company X themselves had been happy with this anonymity for many years, but they are now losing market share because there are more than 150 competitive companies that provide retail solutions. Their previous position as the leading suppliers is not worth very much if people are unaware that it is the case. Company X decided that they needed to re-establish and communicate their position as a market leader.

The sales director at Company X acknowledged that if someone wanted to start a new store, and had no background knowledge, they would not have any obvious way of knowing that Company X was a supplier that had a solution to whatever fitting problems they were trying to solve. Now, Company X is in an unusual position, because they are a large and mature business with an almost nonexistent brand. They are successful, so they have some room to develop. They are being forced to change because of increasing competition in an evolving market. Few other companies would get away with trying to run their business the way that Company X did. The company survived for many years on the strength of their products, without a clear marketing communication strategy. Today, businesses cannot do that, at least not in any existing niche.

Company X first step into improving their market strength to do was a competitor analysis. They needed to know how their competitors are and what markets they serve, so that they can identify threats and weaknesses. From there, they were able to work on their own marketing strategy. Their new marketing strategy involved segmenting the market and picking areas to focus on. They aimed themselves at stores serving the fashion, health and beauty, electronics and convenience markets, as well as grocery stores. These were the segments where they already had a strong presence, and they believed that there was strong growth potential, particularly in fashion, electronics, and health and beauty. With a target audience identified, the next thing they needed to do was build brand awareness with the people who mattered. The first step toward achieving this was to attend trade fairs, so that they could get their products in front of the people who are actually making purchasing decisions. They also made some revamped brochures to hand out at those fairs.

One unusual decision that Company X made was to not actually show any of their products at the trade fairs; they do not have products for people to get a close look at because they know there are industry representatives at the fairs who are only there to look at other people's ideas, with a view to copying them. Instead, they only meet with prospective buyers, and they show them brochures. This may seem like an unconventional viewpoint, but it highlights the fact that the best tactic against competition is constant innovation and renewal. Company X managed to market their offering with a relatively small spend. In the B2B environment, especially with the kind of customers that they are dealing, the important thing is not to reach buyers with glitz and glamor, but to demonstrate that the product is of high quality, and to present facts about the price, the features, etc. The one thing that many companies overlook is that it is important to be consistent with this.

Many B2B marketers see poor ROI because they are inconsistent with their marketing.

References

Argenti, P., Howell, R., & Beck, K. (2005). The strategic communication imperative. *MIT Sloan Management Review, 46*(3), 82–89.

Badaracco, J. L., Jr. (1991). *The knowledge link: How firms compete through strategic alliances.* Boston, MA: Harvard Business School Press.

Ballantyne, D. (1994). Marketing at the crossroads. *Australasian Marketing Journal (Previously Asia Australia Marketing Journal), 2*(1), 1–9. (special issue on relationship marketing).

Christopher, M., Payne, A., & Ballantyne, D. (1991). *Relationship marketing: Bringing quality, customer service and marketing together.* Oxford: Butterworth Heinemann.

Cornelissen, J. (2009). *Corporate communication: A guide to theory and practice* (2nd ed.). Thousand Oaks: Sage.

Ernst, J. (2011, October 26). Metrics that matter for B2B marketers. *Forrester Research.*

Ewing, M. (2009). Integrated marketing communications measurement and evaluation. *Journal of Marketing Communications, 15*(2–3), 103–117.

Grönroos, C. (2000). *Service management and marketing* (2nd ed.). Chichester: Wiley.

Gummesson, E. (2002). Practical value of adequate marketing management theory. *European Journal of Marketing, 36*(3), 325–349.

Gummesson, E. (2004). Return on relationships (ROR): The value of relationship marketing and CRM in business-to-business contexts. *Journal of Business & Industrial Marketing, 19*(2), 136–148.

Håkansson, H., & Snehota, I. (1995). *Developing relationships in business networks.* London: Routledge.

Husted, C., & Reinecke, N. (2009). Improving public sector purchasing. *McKinsey Quarterly, 4*(2): 18–25

Jackson, B. B. (1985, November–December). Building customer relationships that last. *Harvard Business Review*, pp. 120–128.

Kaplan, R. S., & Norton, D. P. (1996). *The balanced scorecard.* Boston, MA: Harvard Business School Press.

Kotler, P. (2003). *Marketing management*(11th ed.). Upper Saddle River, NJ: Prentice Hall.

Lee, D., & Park, C. (2007). Conceptualization and measurement of multidimensionality of integrated marketing communications. *Journal of Advertising Research, 47*(3), 222–236.

McBride, B. (2007). Measuring print advertising. Retrieved from http://www.marketingpower.com/content1292.php.

McDonald, M., Millman, T., & Rogers, B. (1997). Key account management: Theory, practice and challenges. *Journal of Marketing Management, 13,* 737–757.

Minett, S. (2002). B2B marketing: A radically different approach for business-to-business marketers. In *Financial Times Management* (Vol. 10). Harlow: Prentice Hall.

Quinn, F. (1990). *Crowning the customer*. Dublin: O'Brien Press.

Rust, R. T., Zeithaml, V. A., & Lemon, K. N. (2000). *Driving customer equity*. New York, NY: Free Press.

Shaw, R., & McDonald, M. (2000). *Marketing accountability: The new discipline*. Cranfield: Cranfield School of Management.

Varey, R. (2001). *Marketing communication: An introduction to contemporary issues*. Florence, KY: Routledge.

2

Business-to-Business Marketing Communication During Recession

Abstract This chapter refers to the increasing demand for rationalized budgets and underlines the need for a better understanding of the determinants of successful B2B marketing communication campaigns. This is due to the fact that B2B buyers are by default involved in purchasing of high risk and cost; hence, they need accurate information before they make decisions. The authors, thus, argue that marketing communication is one of the most important aspects for B2B organizations, especially during recession, given its contribution to the creation of robust relationships with customers. According to the authors, effective B2B marketing communication should be viewed as an asset; it is an investment for businesses rather than a cost.

Keywords Recession · B2B marketing communications · Relationship marketing

Marketing Communications During Recession

"Half the money I spend on advertising is wasted; the trouble is I don't know which half." By the time Wanamaker's famous quote became popular again, we all knew that recession was here to stay. The beginning

© The Author(s) 2017   **13**
I. Rizomyliotis et al., *Business-to-Business Marketing Communications*,
DOI 10.1007/978-3-319-58783-7_2

of the millennium coincided with the start of the digital evolution, and with it, marketing, and, subsequently promotion, faced an unprecedented change. At the same time, the need to precisely monitor all business activities and report on their return on investment was abruptly regarded as a given. Marketing rapidly became more digital-oriented, more technology-driven and more scientific. Equally, B2B marketing experienced a similar swift toward digitalization with a simultaneous compulsion for even more rationalized budgets measurable results, advanced strategy, thoughtful market research and sophisticated decision-making. Marketing managers had to be intelligent, cost-effective, modern and scientific altogether.

Amid the digital loom, marketing communication, despite being an integral part of contemporary marketing, was not the first sector to feel the evolution of the digital era; still, it was the first to see the consequences of the economic downturn.

The economy's state has a direct bearing on a number of business transactions in a country. During recessions, there is a slump in economic activity, which is accompanied by a decline in business activities in most organizations (Ahmed et al. 2014). Recessions negatively affect the performance of an entire economy, industries and individual organizations, which is because of the surge in the demand for services and products (Calvo-Porral et al. 2016). Recessions also negatively affect the relationship between business partners, which is likely to affect the overall performance of the company (Brooksbank et al. 2015). The majority of organizations react to recessions by downsizing their budget including the marketing budgets. Nevertheless, not all organizations report poor performance during recession since some exhibit exceptional growth and prosperity. These organizations consider recessions as opportunities for strengthening their business, making aggressive investments and outrunning their weaker rivals (Civi 2013). A notable feature of such organizations, especially those in the business-to-business (B2B) market, is that they do not trim their marketing budgets during recession. Business should not sacrifice the significance of customer relationships during recessions as a means of cutting costs (Singh and Dev 2015). This implies that B2B firms should not abandon pursuing customer relationships during recessions; instead, they should adapt them.

Some authors argue that recession provides an ideal opportunity for B2B firms to know their customers better (Civi 2013). Trusted business partners are valued during recession; hence, it is an opportune time to build relationships through marketing communications.

Organizations react to recession by either investing in marketing communications or trimming marketing budgets significantly. Edeling and Fischer (2016) point out that great marketers do not simply recover from the financial crisis; instead, they continually reinvent their marketing strategies and business models during recession to enable them adapt swiftly to the changes in the marketplace. Many marketers agree that organizations should concentrate on gaining knowledge from their customers and providing superior value during recessionary times (Frösén et al. 2016). However, it is surprising that several organizations elect to cut down their marketing expenses during recession despite evidence from past recessions, suggesting that managers who make investments in marketing communications manage to recover from these economic downturns (Green and Peloza 2015). Evidence suggests that, during the past recessions, organizations that opted to spend more on their marketing and research and development (R&D) activities emerged as winners after the recession (Rollins et al. 2014). This observation implies that recession offers an opportunity for innovative organizations to achieve superior business performance.

How organizations reacted to the recent financial crisis, especially with respect to their marketing communications, might shed light on the importance of marketing communications for B2B organizations during recessions. Nevertheless, it is imperative to consider the unique circumstances of the recent financial crisis when compared to the earlier crises. Rollins et al. (2014) explain that markets and organizations are more codependent when compared to 10 years ago, which can be attributed to a number of factors such as the emergence of social networking, the rise of mobile commerce and Internet marketing (Kashmiri and Mahajan 2014), which has altered how customers look for information and how organizations execute their marketing activities. Surveys from the UK and the USA indicate that the bulk of B2B firms reduced their marketing expenditures during the recent financial crisis (Notta and Vlachvei 2015). According to Rollins et al.

(2014), nearly half of telecommunication and high-tech companies cut their marketing expenditures in 2009 by about 8.3%. In 2009, about 60% of B2B companies reduced their marketing budgets as a reaction to the recession (Rollins et al. 2014). The decision by companies to reduce their marketing expenditures during recessionary times is not a phenomenon unique to English or American companies. In Australia, during the 2008–2009 financial crisis, firms altered their marketing priorities toward placing a greater emphasis on short-term sales due to the economic slowdown (Rollins et al. 2014). Overall, there is agreement that the 2009 recession resulted in the most severe budget cuts for marketing activities in the USA and abroad. Thus, economic slowdowns compel markets to be more innovative and smarter.

Just like the case with previous economic recessions, some companies that steadily invested in sales and marketing during the recent economic crisis reported a growth in their market share. Notable examples of companies that sustained their marketing communication activities during the crisis include Target and Wal-Mart in the USA; consequently, they were able to attract new customers (Rollins et al. 2014). The same results can be achieved by B2B firms, especially since they are reliant on building relationships. As organizations make decisions regarding areas of investing their limited resources, recessionary periods offer a unique opportunity for B2B companies to focus on building relationships with their customers.

The recent financial crisis has resulted in a significant change in B2B marketing, especially a shifting resource from the conventional marketing approaches toward e-marketing. During 2010, the largest increase in budgetary allocation among B2B firms was Internet marketing and direct marketing, both online and offline (Nasir 2015). There was a 12.2% increase in online marketing activities in various industries (Rollins et al. 2014). B2B companies often lag behind business-to-consumer (B2C) companies when it comes to integrating social media into their marketing communication strategies (Kashmiri and Mahajan 2014). In most cases, they adopt a wait-and-see approach; thus, they fail to proactively participate in social media.

Moreover, B2B firms are increasingly investing more in social media when compared to consumer companies, which represents a remarkable change in marketing perception since B2B firms have traditionally concentrated on sales (Nickell et al. 2013). This is an indication that B2B companies are increasingly investing in building relationships. It can also be seen that B2B companies are integrating social media as a crucial component of their marketing communications strategies. For example, the Vice President of American Express OPEN and the winner of the 2009 B2B marketer of the year stated that social media is an important tool in B2B marketing (Rollins et al. 2014). An inference that can be derived following the increased usage of social media in B2B marketing after the recent economic recession is that B2B firms are increasingly focusing more on building relationships rather than on sales.

Consistent with the use of social media after the recent recession is the widespread adoption of customer relationship marketing (CRM) in B2B marketing communications. Irrespective of the recession, a significant proportion of B2B organizations invested in CRM. As of 2009, there was an increase in the use of CRM software in B2B companies by 12.5% when compared to the previous year (Rollins et al. 2014). Experts in B2B marketing communications have indicated that the same trend will continue since firms are increasing their investments in marketing assets like CRM. Most B2B businesses are planning to increase their CRM budget after the recession. For many global B2B brands, these investments have paid off as evident by the increase in the brand value of the world's 100 leading brands. Again, this observation suggests that B2B brands are increasing placing more emphasis on building relationships after the recession.

Another notable marketing communication trend that proved useful for B2B companies during the recession is the emphasis on metrics and analytics, which is concerned with converting large quantities of data into knowledge followed by translating this knowledge to valuable marketing insights such as ways of reaching and communicating customers (Parente and Strausbaugh-Hutchinson 2014). These metrics and analytics in B2B marketing communication are geared toward establishing the marketing activities that are useful and valuable to customers. Some marketers have recommended that B2B companies should utilize this knowledge and data to shift their attention away from the conventional measures, such as new sales and revenue, toward customer lifetime value. Although companies have invested considerably in customer data via CRM systems, the majority of organizations underuse what they know regarding their customers (Paul 2015). Overall, it can be seen that the increased use of metrics and analytics in B2B marketing communications is eventually geared toward creating loyal customers; marketing communication has always been one of the key contributors to building and sustaining long-term relationships with B2B customers, and recession has made that notion more obvious than ever.

An Investment Not a Cost

The effects of marketing communications during recession have been vastly explored in the literature. A meta-analysis to assess the effect of marketing expenditures during recessionary times showed the importance of marketing communications during recessions (Nasir 2015). Traditionally, identifying what the firm's existing and prospective customers' value and communicating it effectively can play a critical role in helping organizations in attracting new and retaining existing customers. By using marketing communications, B2B organizations can retain current customers via reminding them the value they offer (Ahmed et al. 2014). Providing better services and products is not sufficient; companies should also focus on communicating the advantages associated with their products/services clearly and compellingly. Nasir (2015) revealed that companies that tend to cut their budgets are more likely to have a long-term focus as well as lack a market orientation. It was also pointed that companies cutting their budgets on marketing communications are at a higher risk of missing out on future profits and sales (Nasir 2015). The same study indicated that firms that spend more on their marketing communications during recession times perform particularly well during and after the recession. Ahmed et al. (2014) also showed a relationship between business performance and advertising expenditures during recessions.

In this respect, studies indicate that increasing or maintaining marketing spending during recessionary periods results in a higher market share, sales growth and profitability when compared to cutting marketing budgets (Frösén et al. 2016). Additionally, it has been found that

B2B companies that trim their marketing expenditures during recession encounter a decline in profits and sales and continue lagging behind firms that maintained marketing spending even after the end of the recession.

Investments in marketing communications during recessionary periods create opportunities for B2B organizations to achieve competitive advantage in returns, market share and sales in the course of competitive advantage. Nickell et al. (2013) classified B2B businesses into those that reduce, maintain or increase marketing budgets during times of recession. They showed that the firms that increased their marketing budgetary allocations in recession were not significantly less profitable in the course of recession when compared to the firms that maintained their budgetary allocations for marketing communications. However, significant differences in profitability were documented between those that maintained or increased their marketing budgets and those that reduced their marketing budgets (Nickell et al. 2013). Moreover, they reported that the profitability of those who cut their market budgets continued to dwindle even after the end of the recession. By contrast, companies that increased their budgets for marketing communications reported a dramatic increase in their profitability after the recovery of the economy. These companies documented a threefold increase in market share following economic recovery (Nickell et al. 2013). Companies that cut their budgets reported a decline in profitability during the recovery period. Those that maintained budgets for marketing increased their profitability, but, nevertheless, they were outperformed by those that increased their budgetary allocations for marketing (Nickell et al. 2013). These findings simply confirm that investments in marketing communications have long-term benefits for the organization even after the recession has ended.

Similarly, there is consistent and strong evidence suggesting that reducing advertising budgets during recession can have damaging effects on sales during and after the economic slowdown (Singh and Dev 2015). Additionally, cutting advertising expenditures does not serve to increase profitability, which is the intended aim of budgetary cuts during recession. Nasir (2015) estimated that advertising during recession has long-term benefits that can last up to 5 years after the recession.

Evidence also exists to show that a relationship exists between customer loyalty and advertising spending during recession. According to Rollins et al. (2014), cutting spending during recession has been reported to lower customer loyalty for both B2C and B2B firms. Specifically, Rollins et al. (2014) denoted that cutting marketing communication budgets could significantly hurt customer bonding and customer loyalty. The overall observation is that downsizing marketing communication budgets during recessions can weaken B2B brands and reduce profitability even after the recession has ended (Paul 2015). In fact, in B2B business, advertising during tough economic times is an indicator that the business is reliable (Nasir 2015). Additionally, increasing marketing communications during recessions provides an opportunity to increase the voice of the firm due to the reduced competitor activity.

In all, it can be seen that the most dominant response by companies to recession is to cut their marketing communication expenses or even their marketing budgets. This shows that most companies view B2B marketing communications as a cost rather than a valuable tool for developing long-term relationships with customers. However, some changes in the B2B marketing approaches have been witnessed as a result of the recession, especially the shift from conventional measures such as sales and revenue generation toward more emphasis on building relationships. This is evident by increased investments in social media marketing and CRM systems by B2B companies. Ultimately, recessionary periods provide an opportunity for proactive B2B companies to enhance their competitive advantage through tailored marketing communications to maintain long-term relations with their customers instead of cutting marketing communications.

References

Ahmed, M. U., Kristal, M. M., & Pagell, M. (2014). Impact of operational and marketing capabilities on firm performance: Evidence from economic growth and downturns. *International Journal of Production Economics, 154*, 59–71.

Brooksbank, R., Subhan, Z., Garland, R., & Rader, S. (2015). Strategic marketing in times of recession versus growth: New Zealand manufacturers. *Asia Pacific Journal of Marketing and Logistics, 27*(4), 600–627.

Calvo-Porral, C., Stanton, J. L., & Lévy-Mangin, J. P. (2016). Is the economic crisis changing marketing strategies? Evidence from the food industry. *Journal of Global Marketing, 29*(1), 29–39.

Civi, E. (2013). Marketing strategies to survive in a recession. *International Journal of Business and Emerging Markets, 5*(3), 254–267.

Edeling, A., & Fischer, M. (2016). Marketing's impact on firm value: Generalizations from a meta-analysis. *Journal of Marketing Research, 53*(4), 515–534.

Frösén, J., Jaakkola, M., Churakova, I., & Tikkanen, H. (2016). Effective forms of market orientation across the business cycle: A longitudinal analysis of business-to-business firms. *Industrial Marketing Management, 52,* 91–99.

Green, T., & Peloza, J. (2015). How did the recession change the communication of corporate social responsibility activities? *Long Range Planning, 48*(2), 108–122.

Kashmiri, S., & Mahajan, V. (2014). Beating the recession blues: Exploring the link between family ownership, strategic marketing behavior and firm performance during recessions. *International Journal of Research in Marketing, 31*(1), 78–93.

Nasir, S. (Ed.). (2015). *Customer relationship management strategies in the digital era.* Hersey, PA: IGI Global.

Nickell, D., Rollins, M., & Hellman, K. (2013). How to not only survive but thrive during recession: A multi-wave, discovery-oriented study. *Journal of Business & Industrial Marketing, 28*(5), 455–461.

Notta, O., & Vlachvei, A. (2015). Changes in marketing strategies during recession. *Procedia Economics and Finance, 24,* 485–490.

Parente, D. S.-H. (2014). *Advertising campaign strategy: A guide to marketing communication plans.* New York, NY: Cengage Learning.

Paul, J. (2015). Masstige marketing redefined and mapped: Introducing a pyramid model and MMS measure. *Marketing Intelligence & Planning, 33*(5), 691–706.

Rollins, M., Nickell, D., & Ennis, J. (2014). The impact of economic downturns on marketing. *Journal of Business Research, 67*(1), 2727–2731.

Singh, A., & Dev, C. S. (2015). Winners and losers during the great recession the positive impact of marketing expenditures. *Cornell Hospitality Quarterly, 56*(4), 383–396.

3

The Current Media Landscape in Business-to-Business Markets

Abstract The traditional B2B marketing communication channels have faced a decline during the economic recession and after the evolution of the digital era. Still, they continue to signify a large share of B2B marketing communication budgets globally. In light of this seeming situation, the authors make an attempt to portray the current B2B media landscape, suggesting that print media may be losing ground to digital tactics, but still represent an important part of the marketing communication mix. Moreover, the chapter offers implications for marketing communication managers and for publishers of trade journals in the B2B sector.

Keywords Traditional media · Digital media · B2B publishers

The Status Quo

The end of the last decade saw a surge of interest in the use of digital media and technology-driven communications. Social media introduced a communication outburst, which has driven marketers to widely use them as the prime marketing communication route in both the

© The Author(s) 2017   **23**
I. Rizomyliotis et al., *Business-to-Business Marketing Communications*,
DOI 10.1007/978-3-319-58783-7_3

B2C and B2B markets. The B2B marketing landscape, extremely heterogeneous as it has always been, is becoming more diverse and complicated led by this accelerating development of digital media channels. Spending in digital marketing has increased year-on-year accounting for the recently displayed growth in overall UK expenditure (Keynote 2012). At the same time, traditional advertising is once again one of the first areas to receive the effect of the economic downturn.

Swift changes involved in content use resulted in change in the both media and advertising landscapes. The impacts have not only affected these areas independently, but the world of B2B as well. For instance, currently, digital advertising is consuming one of the largest shares of the global marketing budget annually. At this rate, digital advertising is equivalent to the trade shows, conferences and other perceived favorite events in the business today (Iveson 2011). With the high-elevated budget on the digital advertising, it is advisable that marketers re-evaluate their strategies concerning their marketing communication efforts. It is evident that B2B marketing is going through a lot of changes and challenges to integrating the digital advertising techniques into the system. The use of digital properties seems an excellent and viable idea in the industrial market (Gill et al. 2013).

The drop in global advertising sales has dictated the introduction of new communication strategies with the use of digital advertising in partnership with print media, in order to enhance the efficiency of B2B companies in times of recession. With the 10.4% of advertising spending realized in the year 2009, there has been a decrease in 2010 and 2011. With the integration of digital advertising, the spending has increased to an annual rate of 2.6% as of 2011. The digital publishing has elevated from a 40 to 50% in online engagement activities, suggesting what is about to happen to the print media landscape in the future. Evaluating the progress of digital publishing, it can be noted that it has increased from 11.8% in 2009 to 29.3% in 2014. This fact has led companies to embrace and employ digital advertising globally due to its perceived merits (Özlük and Cholette 2007).

Digital advertising has been given considerable preference over print media despite the existence of both in big established companies. Big companies might still give print media a chance with small budget allocation, while some small- and medium-sized companies, depending on their operational structure and financial status, have put digital promotion in the heart of their financial plan, leaving no room for the traditional approach. In small or upcoming businesses, print media budgets have shrank as the marketing budget allocation is entirely given to digital activities. And, to the extent that businesses fail to perceive the Internet as an extension of offline operations, they will also fail to see the most revolutionary possibilities of a thoughtful combination of digital and traditional promotional activities.

According to current research, the traditional means of advertising seem not to attract as many customers as initially (Espejo 2010). In as much as it is perceived as the cost-effective approach, B2B companies have, therefore, resorted to digital media (Kumar and Toteja 2012), which has also shown positive results in thoroughly exploring brands. For this reason, digital advertising has dominated the entire marketing world and is perceived to be taking over the print media. This seems reasonable as B2B companies struggle to strengthen their bonds with customers in the market beyond the margins reached by print media. In other words, the print media is not providing adequate room for this kind of bonding despite other factors held constant.

According to the US agency report of January 2015, digital revenue earned amounted to 7.3% and traditional revenue declined to 1.4% in 2014. The B2B companies are trying to form bodies that are informed of what is expected of them. They take the opportunities availed by marketing strategies that can make their objectives a reality. This leaves them with the digital advertising option as the best way to take over the current market and effectively communicate with their customers (Rinallo and Basuroy 2009). To maximize on this, B2B media owners, trade magazines, for example, have majored on the upcoming social networking techniques all over the global market. These companies have employed the use of portals to capture their potential virtual customers. The availability and access to free online information and techniques has eased the advertisers' efforts to produce quality articles. Thus, the virtual users have portrayed their trustworthiness and credibility in enhancing the value added in advertising. Considering these merits on its use, most businesses have secured digital advertising to maintain their communication with their existing customers (Kaiser and Song 2009).

The concentration on digital promotion does seem disproportionately prevalent, however. While the traditional B2B marketing channels, such as print advertising, face a decline due to the economic recession, they still continue to represent one of the largest shares of B2B marketing expenditure in strong global markets (Keynote 2012; Stevenson and Swayne 2011). In light of this seeming situation, it can be inferred that marketers have not abandoned traditional promotion at the expense of the digital media trend. On the contrary, B2B advertising still represents a significant revenue stream for publishers of trade journals and a significant expense for B2B marketers (Stevenson and Swayne 2011). Business publication advertising in the USA generated revenue of $3.73 billion, more than 25% of total B2B advertising expenditures for the year 2006 (Maddox 2007), while according to the advertising association, an increase in spending across all media marketing channels, including traditional print channels, was witnessed in 2015. In simple terms, print media may be losing ground to digital approaches, but still represent an important part of the marketing communication mix.

Print Media Vs. Digital Media

In this regard, despite the considerable diverse changes in the global market, several companies are still reluctant about shifting to digital advertising. So, B2B companies have reported areas of concern despite the compelling force to cross over. Practically, their efforts to explore the global markets have been deterred due to the insecurity feelings in these businesses. Companies have raised issues concerning the security of their intellectual properties that will be exposed online. This sense of insecurity has left some companies in a state of dilemma. Thus, they shift to digital advertising with, in a way, fear of the unknown. Several businesses are bound to move on irrespective of the risks it entails due to the demands of their current business. In this context, most businesses want to cope with the requirement of the business based on the current trends (Dahlén and Edenius 2007).

According to the research, the companies that fully appreciate the digital era are the ones that were first established during this period. Companies established before this period portray unreserved inclination toward shifting into the digital system (Huhmann et al. 2012). Despite the promising factors associated with the digital movements, these companies tend to be cautious in their promotion-related decisions. There are uncertainties crippling in their shifting. Significant doubts are based on their ability to survive in the digital realm. Lack or inadequate security is seen as a significant threat to the promotion plans implemented (Berry 2012).

Likewise, there are many B2B companies that still consider the traditional advertising influential in nature. Therefore, according to the research, they are reluctant in fully accepting the digital means of advertising embraced globally. Some of them, especially the SMEs, still depend entirely on the print media to communicate in the local or global market (Lischka et al. 2014). For these B2B companies, there is no apparent need for any change, as their current approach has worked effectively in establishing national and international brands in their respective markets. Though it is clear that these companies are also faced with the urge to shift to the new forms of communication, it is difficult for their management to mentally perceive that the marketing communication mix allocation in B2B is closely related to the one in B2C. Still, the merits encountered through digital advertising are much numerous to be ignored by a company trying to understand and meet the needs of most clients. Equally, virtual customers seem to dominate even in the B2B world. Thus, digital advertising migration is expected to progress even further in the years to come (Harris 2013).

B2B Publishers

While B2B publishers are trying to set up the strategies on how to redefine the marketplace rules, the need for businesses to employ competitive promotion strategies is more imperative than ever. For the face of the B2B publishing to be total redefined, digital advertising implementation is needed (Mendy 2011). To maintain the high skill settings and in an attempt to ensure that their intended goals are achieved, the businesses have resorted to employing the use of technology and online techniques in a digital platform. This challenge has been dictated by the dynamic changes encountered in the marketplace (Johnston 2012). For example, over the past years in Italy alone, the revenue in printed media has decreased by more than 10%, the turnover in advertising has dropped by 50% and circulation has fallen by 20%. Similarly, in France, print media have also had a drop in circulation, which is expected to reach 29%, by 2015 (Bassanino and Maresca 2014).

The challenge that publishers face is the need to find a balance between digital and traditional operations and resources. Publishing houses need to put forward a plan of dual structures, both to maintain their traditional business model and to implement a second one for digital. What is encouraging is the speed with which they are adapting to the new era of paid online content, and mobile interaction, without sacrificing the quality of content on different platforms. B2B publishers appear to be making the digital transition quickly with Web and ad revenues important contributors, although mobile has so far failed to deliver on revenues. Interestingly enough, print revenues have not declined quite as quickly as expected.

As Carolyn Morgan (2013) suggests: "...publishers were perhaps unduly pessimistic about the prospects for print, or maybe overly optimistic about the growth potential of web and mobile." It is, thus, acknowledged that many publishers use both print media (Stevenson 2007) and digital forms of advertising to remain viable and competitive in the market. In order to effectively adopt new media, they have to demonstrate flexible and a teamwork mind-set. In this regard, they do need to view the digital era as a new field for competition, which is not necessarily blocking their way of doing things (Thrower 2014). The digital format should be utilized in collaboration with the existing forms to accomplish the company's missions and goals. This technology merging has been employed by companies to ensure partnerships and integration of different forms of advertising to fully explore the brand market. In this attempt to merge and integrate various platforms, these companies are faced with the challenge of reconsidering their business models. If they fail to reconcile, one form seems to dominate over the other (Cameron and Haley 2013).

To Print or Not to Print?

Seeking for survival among several emerging competitors in the marketplace, it is necessary to cope with the emerging trends. Therefore, B2B companies have adopted the new emerging trends to merit in the technological world. They have embraced the new marketing communication models to include the digital technology allocating huge budgets to ensure new trends are integrated. Equally, regardless of the overwhelming recognition of social networking as an effective promotion tool, nonetheless, according to the research, print media is still applicable in most companies. Therefore, in as much as digital advertising is taking over the economic world, the print media still represent an important part of the marketing communication mix. While traditional B2B marketing channels continue to represent the largest share of B2B marketing expenditure, what is really critical is to achieve a delicate balance between all meaningful communication routes. Equally, B2B marketing will continue to involve customization, personal interaction and direct methods of communication given that it targets tightly bounded market segments. Nevertheless, even mass communication is needed in a B2B context, in cases where companies seek to establish increased awareness or positive attitude for their brand.

References

Bassanino, A., & Maresca, A. (2014). From print to digital: The changing face of the media. *Performance, 6*(1), 40–45.

Berry, M. (2012). Practitioner book review: Spending advertising money in the digital age—How to navigate the media flow. *Journal of Direct, Data and Digital Marketing Practice, 14*(1), 80–83. doi:10.1057/dddmp.2012.13.

Cameron, G., & Haley, J. (2013). Feature advertising: Policies and attitudes in print media. *Journal of Advertising, 21*(3), 47–55. doi:10.1080/00913367.1 992.10673375.

Dahlén, M., & Edenius, M. (2007). When is advertising? Comparing responses to non-traditional and traditional advertising media. *Journal of*

Current Issues & Research in Advertising, 29(1), 33–42. doi:10.1080/10641 734.2007.10505206.

Espejo, R. (2010). *Advertising* (1st ed.). Detroit: Greenhaven Press.

Gill, K., Mao, A., Powell, A., & Sheidow, T. (2013). Digital reader vs print media: The role of digital technology in reading accuracy in age-related macular degeneration. *Eye, 27*(5), 639–643. doi:10.1038/eye.2013.14.

Harris, J. (2013). Hamish Pringle and Jim Marshall—Spending advertising money in the digital age—How to navigate the media flow. *International Journal of Advertising, 32*(1), 163. doi:10.2501/ija-32-1-163-164.

Huhmann, B., Franke, G., & Mothersbaugh, D. (2012). Print advertising: Executional factors and the RPB Grid. *Journal of Business Research, 65*(6), 849–854. doi:10.1016/j.jbusres.2011.01.006.

Iveson, K. (2011). Branded cities: Outdoor advertising, urban governance, and the outdoor media landscape. *Antipode, 44*(1), 151–174. doi:10.1111/ j.1467-8330.2011.00849.x.

Johnston, S. (2012). Mechanical to digital printing in Scotland: The print employers' organisation. *Business History, 54*(7), 1193–1194. doi:10.1080/ 00076791.2012.687528.

Kaiser, U., & Song, M. (2009). Do media consumers really dislike advertising? An empirical assessment of the role of advertising in print media markets. *International Journal of Industrial Organization, 27*(2), 292–301. doi:10.1016/j.ijindorg.2008.09.003.

Keynote. (2012). B2B marketing report. *Journal of Print Verses Digital Advertising in the Global Market, 6*, 2–7. doi:10.1002/term.1607.

Kumar, S., & Toteja, R. (2012). Print to digital: A study of students' psychosomatic cost in traditional and e-learning. *Procedia—Social and Behavioral Sciences, 67*, 553–560. doi:10.1016/j.sbspro.2012.11.360.

Lischka, J., Kienzler, S., & Mellmann, U. (2014). Can consumption predict advertising expenditures? The advertising-consumption relation before and after the dot-com crisis in Germany. *Advertising & Society Review, 15*(3). doi:10.1353/asr.2014.0014.

Maddox, K. (2007). Top 100 b-2-b Advertisers Increased Spending 3% in '06. *BtoB* September 10, 25.

Mendy, J. (2011). Employees' witnessed presence in changing organisations concerning advertising. *AI & SOCIETY, 27*(1), 149–156. doi:10.1007/ s00146-011-0324-8.

Morgan, C. (2013, July 7). *How digital is changing specialist media.* Retrieved from http://www.inpublishing.co.uk/kb/articles/how_digital_is_changing_specialist_media.aspx.

Özlük, Ö., & Cholette, S. (2007). Allocating expenditures across keywords in search advertising. *Journal of Revenue and Pricing Management, 6*(4), 347–356. doi:10.1057/palgrave.rpm.5160110.

Rinallo, D., & Basuroy, S. (2009). Does advertising spending influence media coverage of the advertiser? *Journal of Marketing, 73*(6), 33–46. doi:10.1509/jmkg.73.6.33.

Stevenson, T. (2007). A six-decade study of the portrayal of African Americans in business print media: Trailing, mirroring, or shaping social change? *Journal of Current Issues & Research in Advertising, 29*(1), 1–14. doi:10.1080/10641734.2007.10505204.

Stevenson, T. H., & Swayne, L. E. (2011). Is the changing status of african americans in the B2B buying center reflected in trade journal advertising? *Journal of Advertising, 40*(4), 101–122

Thrower, E. (2014). Print and digital media review. *Gastroenterology, 146*(5), 1424–1425. doi:10.1053/j.gastro.2014.03.024.

4

Business-to-Business Print Ad Effectiveness: Some Empirical Evidence

Abstract This chapter attempts to assess the impact of various factors and characteristics on B2B advertising effectiveness. The main focus of the authors is print ad effectiveness given the lack of adequate relevant research and the concurrent need for economical and efficient use of the traditional tools that are reported to be losing ground against digital ones. While there is no doubt that advertising is becoming increasingly important in B2B, managers are becoming more skeptical about the use of print media, partly because of the absence of immediate results and apparent merits deriving from B2B print advertising. As such, the authors aim to contribute to the extant literature by offering some empirical data and some suggestions on how to increase print advertising effectiveness in B2B.

Keywords Industrial print ad · Effectiveness · Print ad campaigns · Attitude toward the ad · Print ad characteristics

© The Author(s) 2017
I. Rizomyliotis et al., *Business-to-Business Marketing Communications*,
DOI 10.1007/978-3-319-58783-7_4

The Importance of Measuring Print Ad Effectiveness

The rapidly changing B2B landscape, driven by the shrinking of marketing budgets, and the increasing demand for measurable results are not paving the way toward an imprudent drop of print media. On the contrary, they are simply highlighting the need for increased accountability of their use. In recognition of the aforementioned need, it is essential for researchers to concentrate on discovering the ways to effectively use print media.

Advertisements have always been dominating marketing communication investments, although companies have a variety of ways to engage their audience, i.e., word of mouth, sales force interaction, trade shows and sales promotion (Chattopadhyay and Laborie 2005). As far as print communications are concerned, over the last five decades, marketers have made great effort and progress in delivering work of high quality with respect to improving the understanding of advertising effectiveness (McBride 2007).

In comparison with the research devoted to consumer advertising, very few studies have been directed toward the effectiveness of industrial advertising. As a matter of fact, the role of advertising in B2B markets has always been regarded with uncertainty (Hanssens and Weitz 1980), in view of the absence of an apparent merit of industrial advertising. On the other hand, advertising is becoming an increasingly important part of industrial marketing programs (Belch and Belch 2009). As such, industrial marketers are investigating the use of economical and efficient communication vehicles in order to support the traditionally emphasized but relatively expensive tool of personal selling (Shimp 2007).

The growing importance of industrial advertising underlines the need for a better understanding and further research of the determinants of a successful print ad. The resulting prescriptions for enhanced industrial print ads have focused on various aspects of effectiveness, from the investigation of ad effectiveness measurement to the identification of specific elements, such as headlines, text and layout characteristics, having an impact on effectiveness (Lohtia et al. 1995).

Still, the need for additional research on industrial print advertising is evident, given the relative lack of research in the B2B area. In light of this seeming situation, just as the dimensions of the "ideal" ad have yet to be discovered, correspondingly, no single measure of ad effectiveness has yet received endorsement as the most appropriate measure of print ad effectiveness.

Consequently, the main objective of this study is to assess the link between industrial print ad effectiveness and print ad characteristics, by exploring the relative importance of various print ad characteristics with respect to their impact on various measures of effectiveness. By understanding the way the various ad characteristics can enhance the effectiveness of a print ad, business marketers should be able to create a more effective ad. The important and challenging task of exploring the linkage between advertising effectiveness and its determinants is clearly depicted by McBride (2007): "The real world of stimulus (the ad)—response (the action of the target) is complicated to measure because human reaction isn't always predictable and because people are rarely exposed to a stimulus in a vacuum. Well-designed print research can, however, identify whether an ad has the elements that should make it effective in the marketplace as well as determine what and how it communicates."

In the following sections, a thorough review of the studies conducted in the print ad effectiveness area will be presented and the conceptual framework of the study together with the methodology used in order to meet our objectives will be discussed. Following the presentation and discussion of the research findings, the limitations of this study along with the suggestions for future research are highlighted.

In order to get a better understanding of the print ad effectiveness in the B2B market, we conducted 2 studies. We contacted both (a) businesses that advertise their products or services through print ads and (b) businesses that receive and process print adverts. In other words, in the first study, we included businesses that have created print ad campaigns in order to promote their products to other businesses; they provided us with info on the dimensions of a successful print ad campaign. The second group comprises managers that receive and process print ads, as they are the ones to receive other businesses' promotion on behalf of their company. They have provided us with information on the key aspects of an effective print ad from a B2B reader (and of course buyer) point of view.

Study 1: Industrial Print Ad Characteristics and Their Impact on Print Ad Effectiveness

This study attempts to contribute to the research undertaken in the field of industrial advertising. Using data from 350 B2B companies from Italy, Greece and Cyprus, the study explores the factors that influence the outcome of B2B advertising campaigns in print media. The relative importance of all, but one, of those factors, varies depending on whether the communication goal of the campaign is to increase sales, create awareness or favorable attitude toward the advertised product. Only the relationship between the company and the advertising agency was found to be an important factor regardless of the communication goal of the company.

Study 1 Background and Conceptual Framework

Many theories have been elaborated regarding the way consumers deal with advertising (Craik and Lockhart 1972; Baker 2000; Leigh et al. 2006), and their existence goes back to the last decade of the nineteenth century, when the effect of advertising was examined as a result of sales force interaction (Briggs 2006). The extant literature on print advertising which is mostly dealing with copy testing, media research and campaign assessment research (Wimmer and Dominick 2006), is also predominantly concerned with the investigation of consumer ads. In this context, a number of studies have assessed the relationship between effectiveness and characteristics of ads appearing in consumer publications (e.g., Diamond 1968; Silk and Geiger 1972; Troldahl and Jones 1965; Fletcher and Zeigler 1978; Holbrook and Lehmann 1980; Finn 1988; Bendixen 1993; Toncar and Munch 2001).

In more recent studies, various approaches were used in order to explore print adverts and their effectiveness on consumer behavior. Bansal and Gupta (2014) studied the psychological influence of the newspaper advertisement on the behavior and attitude of modern consumers. They provide a comparison of the customer perception of a newspaper advertisement versus the intended perception. The authors state that perception and psychological are vital as they tend to affect consumer behavior. They used Resnik and Stern criteria to evaluate the ad information level of the newspaper advertisement. The research results indicate that most ads were informative. The study of Cengiz et al. (2011) discusses the influence of source likeability and credibility on the print advertisement effectiveness. The authors provide a theoretical model that can be used to represent the influence of source characteristics on the band and advertisement attitude, as well as the customers' desire to buy. The research findings indicate that the relationship sequence between the purchase willingness, source characteristics and attitudinal responses may vary substantially due to different levels of motivation and product awareness.

Similarly, Estéve and Fabrizio (2014) investigate the effectiveness of advertising in terms of consumers' and advertisers' needs. The authors make an emphasis on the brand image, recalling and purchasing intention. They develop a benchmark advertising effectiveness measure to help businesses increase their profits.

The essential role of advertising in the product and service promotion is also discussed by Keshari et al. (2013). The authors state that advertising is an integral communication part of marketing as it helps to sell the products and contribute to the image development. They try to explore the factors that ensure the service advertising effectiveness.

Nayak and Shah (2015) further explore advertising as a communication form that aims at persuading customers to buy or consume the goods. Despite the existence of new advertising methods, the importance of print advertisement is not obsolete, they suggest. Many businesses use newspaper print ads to promote their brands and influence brand building, as they help customers make proper purchase decisions. The authors base their research on the effectiveness survey of newspaper print ads. Print advertising and its importance in contemporary small- and medium-sized businesses is also discussed by Novak-Marcincin et al. (2012). The authors analyze the case of SME's enterprise X to reveal the truth about advertising performance and its role. Also, they discuss the effectiveness of ads and their contribution to the business development in different markets. According to their research, although many enterprises still use ads to promote their products and services, there are numerous companies which would never apply this tool.

The issue of print advertising effectiveness is also addressed by Olsen et al. (2012). Using a survey to collect the research data, they suggest that "white space" format is effective to advertise product brands rather than services. Also, it was found to increase attention to the overall advertisement. Finally, it conveys brand prestige and focuses customers' attention on the product and brand name. Printhvi and Dash (2013) conducted a comparative study to assess the effectiveness of radio, print and Web advertising and emphasize that some types of adverts are not given proper importance. The authors highlight that print advertising is still effective in changing attitudes.

In addition, Baack et al. (2015) state that B2B advertising research presupposes the investigation of functional, factual and benefit-laden messages. However, they indicate that creativity is vital to any advertising, print one in particular. The research results indicate that message creativity has a substantial influence on the response of business managers. Also, creative ads impact the attitude toward the brand, intentions and the ad itself. They conclude that the creativity role is immense in B2B advertising and show ways to improve the effectiveness of print ads in B2B.

Sinha et al. (2012) cover the issue of B2B advertising and related rational and emotional appeals as well. The authors investigate the use of advertising for B2B products and services with the use of research data from both trade journals and print ads.

Terkan (2014) addresses the use of creativity in print advertising in the modern business world. The author suggests that creative advertising is essential for a business to business as it enables to get a deep insight into the effective work of both producers and sales companies. The author states that advertising becomes more relevant in business to business than ever and suggests that it is now vital for businesses to adopt creative strategies and innovations to survive increased competition and challenges.

Findings coming from the comparison of business-to-business advertising in different countries are explored with respect to their communication styles and the impact of national culture on franchise recruitment in the work of Wason et al. (2014). The authors state that the style plays an essential role in B2B ads; thus, to make an effective print advertising, it is important to choose the most appropriate communication dimensions and styles.

Table 4.1 Advertisement readership measurement

Types of ad readership measures	What do they measure?
Starch scores	They measure recall and readership of an ad providing indication of the percentage of readers who have noticed, seen/associated and read most of an ad
Ad–chart scores	They measure recall and readership of an ad providing indication of the percentage of readers who have noted, started to read and read half or more of an ad
Ad–sell scores	They measure whether an ad is able to be noticed, to arouse interest or keep customers sold

Nevertheless, the research that focuses on the way visual elements relate to print ad effectiveness has been limited (McQuarrie 2005). Indeed, very few studies, published more than 20 years ago, have been directed at the effectiveness of B2B print ads examining a wide range of print ad characteristics and their impact on various measures of print ad effectiveness.

Specifically, Assael et al. (1967) using the ad–chart scores (see Table 4.1) of ad effectiveness—explained the variance related to recall and readership of industrial ads examining characteristics such as color or illustration and suggested that bleed page and the shape of illustration were important for attracting attention to the ad, whereas copy length, headline and color were important for improving readership measures. Also, Hanssens and Weitz (1980) demonstrated that industrial ad effectiveness is related to format and content characteristics of the ad. The authors used the starch scores (see Table 4.1) and the number of inquiry calls to measure print ad effectiveness and found that the size of text had little impact on ad effectiveness, whereas photographs and illustrations enhanced ad recall and readership.

Furthermore, the study by Soley and Reid (1983a) that used the ad–chart scores has shown that the shape of the photograph improves ad recall. Also, after examining headline characteristics, they showed that the number of phrase units in the headline positively affects readership.

However, a similar study again by Soley and Reid (1983b), using the ad–chart scores as the print ad effectiveness measurement, suggested that no specific type of headline is significant for predicting readership. Zinkhan (1984) concentrated his research on the effectiveness of the ad content with respect to the reader's attitude toward the ad highlighting the importance of the ad text. Likewise, Chamblee and Sandler (1992) investigated the impact of various ad layout styles on ad effectiveness as measured by the ad—sell scores (see Table 4.1) and found that the most effective style was that of the copy being wrapped around the illustration. Multiple illustrations were shown to be more effective than a single one, while long copies were found to have better effects than short ones.

Finally, Lohtia et al. (1995) linked specific ad content characteristics to various dimensions of ad effectiveness and highlighted the importance of content characteristics by suggesting a thorough presentation of the product and its benefits in the ad.

A selection of research findings on industrial print advertising pertinent to this study is presented in Table 4.2.

Following the review of what is known about print ad effectiveness, it can be noted that there is no explicit prescription for an effective ad and that the effect of various characteristics may differ depending on the intended objective and the respective measure. It is clear, thus, that more research should be carried out with respect to the linkage between particular measures of print ad effectiveness and print ad characteristics.

So far, the measurement of effectiveness has included such measures as attention, awareness, recall, recognition, readership, inquiry generation or even sales (Wimmer and Dominick 2006). No formal approaches, however, have been developed to examine the effectiveness of industrial print ad using a broader set of measures. Consequently, our study integrates previous findings with a new approach testing for the first time the importance of a specific set of variables of all three groups of ad characteristics, i.e., layout, content and headline, across a wide range of selected measures of industrial ad effectiveness, namely recall, readership, attitude toward the ad and persuasion.

It is, thus, the intention of this study to gain a better understanding of industrial print effectiveness, by taking into consideration a combination of the most critical measures, instead of using a sole measure of ad effectiveness. With respect to this comprehensive approach, it is expected that the determination of the impact of certain ad characteristics on ad effectiveness will lead to some significant empirical results. Figure 4.1 presents the conceptual framework of this study.

Table 4.2 Industrial print ad: selected research findings

Studies	Findings
Assael et al. (1967)	Bleed page and the shape of illustration are important for attracting attention to the ad
	Copy length, headline and color are improving readership measures
Hanssens and Weitz (1980)	Photographs increase ad effectiveness in routine and basic products
	Copy size increases effectiveness for unique and routine products but not for important products
Soley and Reid (1983a, b)	Larger pictures and less copy are related to ad effectiveness
	Product picture is not significant for ad effectiveness
Zinkhan (1984)	Ad effectiveness can be measured with use of 5 dimensions: cognitive, affective, personal relevance, humor and familiarity. The first three are related to behavioral intention
Chamblee and Sandler (1992)	Long copy is more effective than short copy
	Multiple illustrations are more effective than single
Lohtia et al. (1995)	Content characteristics are important regarding the ad effectiveness since they present the product and its benefits in the ad

Study1 Methodology Results and Discussion

In order to meet the objectives of the study, data were collected regarding print ads from well-known industrial magazines in Italy, Greece and Cyprus. All print ads that appeared in B2B magazines were used in the study. Cooperation was secured for marketing managers who were readers of magazines as well as potential B2B buyers of the products presented in the print ads. These managers were contacted and were asked to indicate the ads that were more effective with respect to each measure used by the authors.

In order to assess the ***effectiveness of a print ad,*** we used four criteria: ad recall, ad readership, attitude toward the ad and persuasion from the ad. *Ad recall* can be measured by defining the number of people who remember the ad at a later point in time (Leigh et al. 2006; Stapel 1998). Ad recall was measured using the ad–chart scores that, among others, represent the percentages of respondents who noted the print

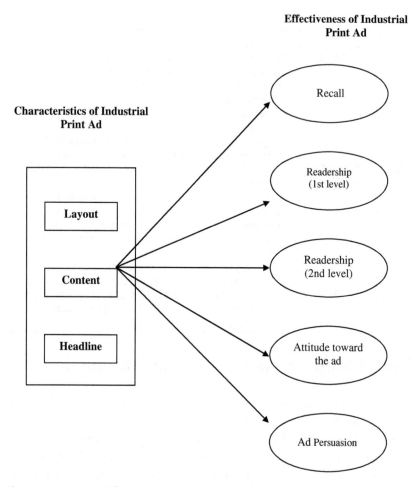

Fig. 4.1   Conceptual framework of Study 1

ad. The specific method was selected since it is a very objective method to measure the effectiveness of a print ad (Wells 2000). Although recall is commonly used as an effectiveness measure, it has some weaknesses (Wells 2000). This fact together with the need of assessing a more dynamic view of ad effectiveness led us to use other evaluation tools as well, namely readership, attitude toward the ad and persuasion. Ad readership was measured using the ad–chart scores. Accordingly, the subscribers were asked to indicate whether they have started to read (readership 1st level) or read half or more (readership 2nd level) of the print ad. The respondents were asked to indicate their attitude toward the ad using the 3 item 5-point Likert scale developed by Kamp and McInnis (1995). Finally, in order to measure the ad persuasion effect, the respondents were asked to answer the question of how likely they were to try the product. This question is used in starch-like technique in order to demonstrate the probability of eventually buying the advertised product using a 5-point Likert scale. The pertinent statistics of all dependent variables of the study are shown in Table 4.3.

Ad Characteristics

The set of characteristics included in the study was developed after following specific steps. First of all, we carried out a thorough review of the pertinent published work to identify the characteristics that are examined in the literature. Then, we conducted a series of interviews with both advertising executives and industrial publishers, in order to identify the present status of print advertising in Greece. Finally, five academics specializing in advertising assisted us in forming the appropriate set of characteristics to be used in the specific research. The set of characteristics included in our study were grouped into three categories, namely layout characteristics, content characteristics and headline characteristics. Each characteristic has taken the value of 0 or 1 by the researchers depending on its existence (1) or otherwise (0) in the 100 ads studied (see Table 4.4).

In order to identify the most effective characteristics of industrial print advertising, five separate multiple regression analyses were carried out, one for each measure of print ad effectiveness, i.e., recall, readership (1st level), readership (2nd level) and attitude toward the ad and ad persuasion.

Table 4.3 Operationalization of dependent variables

Ad effectiveness approach	Measurement	Mean		Standard deviation		Crombach a
Recall	Number of respondents (%) who noted the ad	22.09%		–		–
Readership (1st level)	Number of respondents (%) who started to read the ad	16.71%		–		–
Readership (2nd level)	Number of respondents (%) who read half or more of the ad	7.47%		–		–
Attitude toward the ad	1. Overall, what is your impression of this ad? 5-point Likert (Disliked it very much, Liked it very much)	2.619	**3.276** (3-item scale)	0.388	**0.534** (3-item scale)	**0.928**
	2. To what degree did you feel positively toward this ad? 5-point Likert (Not at all positive, Very positive)	3.134		0.544		
	3. Overall, how well did you like this ad? 5-point Likert (Did not like it at all, Liked it very much)	3.674		0.744		
Ad persuasion	How likely are you to try the product? 5-point Likert (Very likely, Very unlikely)	2.468		0.538		–

Table 4.4 Ad characteristics used in the study

Ad characteristics	Appearance in the ad	
Layout	*No*	*Yes*
There is a photograph of the product in the ad	45%	55%
Other illustration in the ad	46%	54%
The trademark of the company appears in the ad	43%	57%
The product appears in action	57%	43%
Multiple products shown in the ad	53%	47%
Content	*No*	*Yes*
There are product specification in the copy	50%	50%
There are tangible statements about the product	32%	68%
There is a slogan in the ad	40%	60%
There is a promise for a benefit in the ad	49%	51%
The name of the company is underlined in the ad	55%	45%
Headline	*No*	*Yes*
The headline is interrogative	52%	48%
There are more than 5 words in the headline	46%	54%
The product name or the company name is mentioned in the headline	67%	33%
There is a product feature or a benefit feature in the headline	59%	41%

Table 4.5 Multiple regression results (dependent variable: recall)

Variable	Standardized beta	t statistics	Sig.
(constant)		7.820	0.000
There is a photograph of the product in the ad	0.781	11.364	0.000
Other illustration in the ad	0.503	7.814	0.000
The product appears in action	−0.310	−4.830	0.000

$R^2 = 0.628$
Durbin–Watson = 2.220
$F = 53.227$/Sig. = 0.000

Recall

The results of this multiple regression analysis, which are shown in Table 4.5, indicate that the regression model is significant at 0.01 level. The model suggests that recall is affected by layout characteristics. Specifically, if the goal of the company is to increase print ad recall, then

Table 4.6 Multiple regression results (dependent variable: readership—1st level)

Variable	Standardized beta	t statistics	Sig.
(constant)		−0.598	0.552
There is a promise for a benefit in the ad	0.571	9.503	0.000
There is a slogan in the ad	0.348	5.771	0.000
There are tangible statements about the product	0.312	5.483	0.000
The product appears in action	0.303	5.294	0.000

$R^2 = 0.726$
Durbin–Watson $= 1.882$
$F = 54.814$/Sig. $= 0.000$

the communication manager should create an ad that contains an illustration and a photograph of the advertised product. These results are consistent with the findings of previous work done by Soley and Reid (1983a, b) and Chamblee and Sandler (1992). These findings illustrate the reader's need to have a visual perception of an ad in order to be able to recall it. Nevertheless, the company should avoid showing the product in action.

Readership

The results (Table 4.6) indicate that the company should place a slogan in the ad in order to increase the number of the readers who start reading the ad (readership 1st level). Moreover, the probability of achieving this advertising goal increases to the extent that the ad contains tangible statements for the advertised product, a finding which is supported by the work done by Hanssens and Weitz (1980).

Likewise, with respect to this specific effectiveness measure, it is important to show the advertised product in action together with a promise of a benefit resulting from the usage of the product. As we can see, readership is mostly affected by content factors, a finding which is consistent with all previous empirical results (Hanssens and Weitz 1980; Chamblee and Sandler 1992; Soley and Reid 1986). This underlines the

Table 4.7 Multiple regression results (dependent variable: readership—2nd level)

Variable	Standardized beta	t statistics	Sig.
(constant)		−1.040	0.333
There is a product or a benefit feature in the headline	0.328	5.918	0.000
There is a slogan in the ad	0.324	3.910	0.000
There is a promise for a benefit in the ad	0.216	2.413	0.022
There are tangible statements about the product	0.192	2.305	0.044

$R^2 = 0.411$
Durbin–Watson = 2.000
$F = 17.113$/Sig. = 0.000

fact that industrial customers tend to seek more product information usually conveyed through ad text.

The results of the regression analysis reported in Table 4.7 suggest that the mention of a product feature in the headline has a positive impact on readership (2nd level). In addition, it can be inferred that the ad tends to have higher readership when backed up with specific, tangible statements. These results are consistent with the study carried out by Hanssens and Weitz (1980) which indicated the positive effect of product specifications for routine and unique products. Likewise, it is important to use a slogan and a promise for a benefit in order to keep the customers interested and eventually motivate them to read the entire ad. In other words, in order to motivate customers to read the entire ad in addition to aforementioned content characteristics, the ad should include a product feature or benefit feature in the headline.

Attitude Toward the Ad

The results of this multiple regression analysis, which are shown in Table 4.8, indicate that the characteristics which contribute to the creation of a positive attitude toward the ad, and representing all three categories of characteristics of the study, are photograph of the product, promise for a benefit and product or benefit feature in the headline.

Table 4.8 Multiple regression results (dependent variable: attitude toward the ad)

Variable	Standardized beta	t statistics	Sig.
(constant)		26.667	0.000
There is a photograph of the product in the ad	0.268	2.911	0.002
There is a promise for a benefit in the ad	0.278	3.013	0.002
There is a product or a benefitfeature in the headline	0.185	1.996	0.049

$R^2 = 0.242$
Durbin–Watson = 1.522
$F = 9.028$/Sig. = 0.000

Table 4.9 Multiple regression results (dependent variable: ad persuasion)

Variable	Standardized beta	t statistics	Sig.
(constant)		28.881	0.000
There is a promise for a benefit in the ad	0.413	4.233	0.000

$R^2 = 0.112$
Durbin–Watson = 1.519
$F = 7.092$/Sig. = 0.000

These characteristics are expected to lead readers to adopt a favorable attitude toward the ad. A possible reason underlying this finding is that the ad that provides an evident, visualized and justified reason for selecting a product is more close to gain the positive attitude of an industrial reader.

Ad Persuasion

The results of the regression analysis presented in Table 4.9 indicate that only the promise of a benefit in the ad is significantly and positively related to increasing the persuasive power of the ad. Nevertheless, this effect is relatively weak. One possible explanation of this is the fact that due to the dominant role of personal selling in the B2B buying process, a B2B customer is not expected to solely give credit to the persuasive effect of an ad during a purchase.

The results lead to some very interesting and important conclusions that may be useful to the industrial marketing executives. First of all, the impact of the characteristics studied in this research depends on the measure used to evaluate print ad effectiveness. Thus, ad recall is solely dependent on layout characteristics, whereas ad persuasion appears to be affected only by content characteristics (i.e., promise for a benefit). Creating visual allure through photographs of the product or other illustration is important for creating ads that are noticeable and easy to remember. The visuals, though, should be immediately relevant to the target audience or else the implementation of a certain layout would not lead to the desired results.

Nevertheless, the company should be cautious when presenting the product in action since the usage of this characteristic seems to have a negative effect on recall, while at the same time, it enhances readership. A possible reason for this is probably the fact that showing a product in action to readers who are interested in the ad will eventually lead them to read a big proportion of the ad. Industrial readers, in particular, tend to seek details for the advertised products since the industrial buying process is by nature a complicated procedure based on many buying criteria and the examination of specific aspects of the products. In this context, the existence of additional information, such as the appearance of a product in action, can offer an incentive for a reader who is interested, to read an ad.

Moreover, the examination of the way that all 3 measures of effectiveness are affected by the name of the company or the product led to a very interesting finding regarding the very delicate matter of branding in industrial markets. According to our results, when the trademark or the name of the company or the product appears in the ad, there is no significant impact on print ad effectiveness. Actually, branding research has largely focused on consumer goods markets and only recently has attention been given to business markets (Cretu and Brodie 2007). A small number of studies have focused on the examination of branding (Mudambi et al. 1997; Mudambi 2002; Lynch and de Chernatony 2004), and most of them have actually underlined its importance in industrial markets (Shipley and Howard 1993; Cretu and Brodie 2007), stating, though, the need for further research into the way in which brands are communicated in B2B markets.

In addition, Saunders and Watt (1979) argued that branding alone is unlikely to be of value in the market. While branding has significant importance to consumer enterprises, it has virtually small relevance to B2B companies, where buying decisions are made by a group of people. Industrial buyers are rational decision-makers who are not influenced by emotional factors such as brands and that is why industrial marketing has always communicated tangible product features to prospects. In other words, the fundamental way of establishing bondage with customers is primarily based on good personal selling, since purchases are usually based on face-to-face interactions between the buyer and the sales representative. By virtue of these facts, B2B buyers are not expected to be primarily influenced by the brand name of the company stated in the ad, but instead, they tend to be interested in more specific and tangible elements such as price, quality and availability.

Furthermore, according to our results, both readership measures are strongly related to content factors. The weak relationship between layout and readership may occur because information is usually conveyed through the ad text. Consequently, if the company aims at the creation of effective ads with regard to high readership, then the incorporation of a slogan, a promise of a benefit and tangible product specifications appear to be necessary.

Finally, if the goal is to enhance effectiveness in terms of creating positive attitude toward the ad, the company should pay more attention in visualizing the product and emphasizing the benefits emerging from the product usage, in both the text and the headline. In sum, this study strengthens previous research findings regarding the delicate balance to be achieved between the print ad characteristics. In any case, management is in better position to make any trade-off decisions, armed with an indication of the impact of every decision on print ad effectiveness.

Study 2: An Exploratory Study of the Factors Influencing the Successful Outcome of Industrial Print Ad Campaigns

Over the years, a great deal of research has been undertaken on consumer advertising, whereas little attention has been directed toward industrial advertising. Industrial marketers have traditionally placed most of their communication emphasis on personal selling and have always faced problems convincing top managers of the value of advertising due to lack of actual proof that advertising is effective in B2B markets (Donovan 1979). Nevertheless, the development of more sophisticated communication management skills, the broader understanding of the industrial buyer and the development of worldwide markets (Havens 1980) have contributed to the sharp increase in the importance of business-to-business advertising.

However, few empirical studies indicate how to create successful advertising campaigns (e.g., Korgaonkar et al. (1986)). Given the large sums of money spent on industrial advertising and the dominant role of print ads on the advertising plan, the need for more research on the determinants of a successful print ad campaign is obvious and highlights the importance of this study. What is more print ads and the identification of the parameters of an effective print ad campaign is a field that, to the best of our knowledge, very little research has been done so far. Consequently, the resulting objectives of this study were as follows: a) to investigate the factors that influence the outcome of print advertising activities and b) to explore the relative importance of those factors with respect to the intended outcome of the campaign.

Study 2 Background and Conceptual Framework

Increased attention to the industrial communication activities has encouraged the evaluation of the use and the relative importance of various promotional tools (Parasuraman 1981). Topics such as publicity (Williams 1983), trade shows (Cavanaugh 1976) and direct mail

(Ljungren 1976) have been studied and evaluated in terms of their impact on sales volume. On the other hand, since business advertising usually bears no direct relationship to specific sales volume targets, attempts have been made in the literature to examine its supporting role in the communication strategy of a B2B company. Specifically, Morrill (1970) studied the impact of B2B advertising on salesperson effectiveness, and he found that the sales achieved per salesperson call were significantly higher when customers had been exposed to advertising.

In recent works, Maheshwari et al. (2014) analyze the measures of advertisement effectiveness critically reviewing a number of previous studies on the effectiveness of advertising. The authors suggest that although technology has substantially changed the way businesses promote their products and services, traditional advertising is still popular and they discuss the ways companies use it to improve and upgrade themselves to meet the demands and expectations of their current and potential customers. Feld et al. (2012) compare the effectiveness of print advertising with TV and direct main advertising campaigns. Hence, they suggest that print ads, together with other advertisement types, enable to create brand awareness and are effective for business to business. According to the research, print advertisements are stimuli exposures that generate contact with the recipients of the advertising campaigns.

Jensen and Jepsen (2007) provide a critical description of low attention processing, demonstrating the application of the suggested framework. They apply a content analysis to collect the research data and research the emotional appeals used in different types of ads to target the selected market. At the same time, LaPlaca (2013) investigates the effect of branding and advertising on B2B marketing and provides numerous research topics and extended literature review, indicating on the B2B aspects that are of high importance.

Pieters et al. (2007) investigate the ways to optimize the ads to make them effective for business to business. An emphasis is made on the influence of design elements and size on the effectiveness of an advertising campaign. Also, the study by Yoon and Kijewski (1995) has shown that buyers who had been exposed to a supplier's advertisement rated the supplier's sales personnel substantially higher on product knowledge, service and enthusiasm. In addition to enhancing sales effectiveness and forming positive buyer attitude, business advertising often creates awareness of the supplier and the supplier's products. In a study by Herzog (1985), 61% of the design engineers returning an inquiry card from a magazine ad indicated that they were unaware of the company that advertised before seeing the ad.

Still, it is clear that industrial advertising should be evaluated more in terms of the intended communication goals, such as brand awareness, buyer attitude, recognition, provision of information and generation of important leads for salesperson, rather than solely in terms of sales or profits (Smith and Swinyard 1982). In this context, Korgaonkar et al. (1986) attempted to identify the factors that determine successful industrial advertising in terms of increasing sales, creating a positive attitude and increasing awareness. The factors that the authors examined were product uniqueness, competition, agency and client relationships, market research, resources, media selection, message and creativity. They found that the impact of the factors related to successful industrial advertising campaigns in general vary according to the intended objectives of the campaign. This study follows Korgaonkar et al. (1986) approach, and Fig. 4.2 shows the conceptual framework. However, this study focuses specifically on industrial print ad campaigns and uses data referring to specific ads rather than to any ads that respondents might have in mind.

Study 2 Methodology Results and Discussion

In order to meet the objectives of the study, data were collected from local B2B companies in Italy, Greece and Cyprus, as again they were the ones to first feel the effects of recession in the European Union. A total of 300 print ad campaigns were included in the study for which cooperation was secured on behalf of the companies that had designed theses specific advertising campaigns. Personal interviews were conducted with the personnel responsible for the ad campaigns in question, usually marketing managers, communication managers, product managers and sales managers. A research instrument was designed and was tested

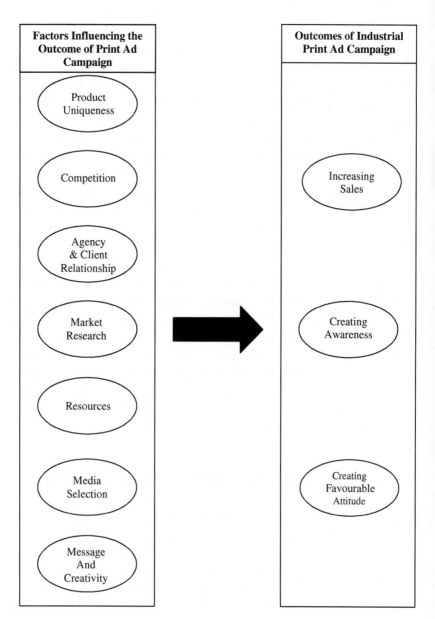

Fig. 4.2   Conceptual framework of Study 2

Table 4.10 Operationalization and evaluation of the dependent variables of the study

Dependent variables	Statements	Reliability coefficient alpha
Degree of success in terms of sales	The print ad campaign was successful in generating new sales The print ad campaign was successful in increasing sales of the advertised product	0.962
Degree of success in terms of attitude	The print ad campaign was successful in terms of developing positive attitude toward the advertised product The print ad campaign was successful in developing liking for the advertised product	0.925
Degree of success in terms of awareness	The print ad campaign was successful in terms of generating awareness The print ad campaign was successful in terms of getting attention	0.948

with the help of 10 academics and numerous practitioners with a good knowledge in this specific research area.

The respondents were asked to indicate their agreement or disagreement using a 5-point Likert scale to a number of statements adopted from the scales and developed by Korgaonkar et al. (1986) to measure dependent variables of our model, namely the degree of success in terms of sales, attitude and awareness. A description of the dependent variables is presented in Table 4.10.

Moreover, the set of independent variables included in the study, namely the set of factors influencing the outcome of the campaign (33 items), was also developed by Korgaonkar et al. (1986) and was adopted to meet the objectives of the study. A description of the independent variables, pertaining to product uniqueness, competition, agency and client relationships, market research, resources, media selection, message and creativity, is presented in Table 4.11.

Table 4.11 Evaluation of the independent variables of the study

Factors	CMIN	GFI	TLI	CFI	RMSEA	AVE	CFR
Product uniqueness	69.037	0.903	0.977	0.984	0.076	0.563	0.830
Competition	39.923	0.924	0.970	0.979	0.078	0.567	0.831
Agency and client relationships	24.959	0.944	0.985	0.991	0.062	0.758	0.902
Market research	24.959	0.944	0.985	0.991	0.062	0.714	0.921
Resources	2.221	0.990	0.996	0.999	0.033	0.854	0.959
Media selection	3.865	0.985	0.996	0.999	0.054	0.811	0.955
Message and creativity	69.037	0.903	0.977	0.984	0.076	0.825	0.974

Unlike Korgaonkar et al. (1986), we carried out a factor analysis in order not only to identify the structure of the factors that derived from the aforementioned 33 items but also to confirm our model.

Consequently, in addition to exploratory factor analysis (EFA), we also carried out confirmatory factor analysis (CFA). The usage of CFA was thought to be of great importance in this study since the theoretical expectations regarding the structure of our data were strong enough. Many studies have underlined the importance of using both EFA and CFA, depending on the nature of the data, since each method provides different type of information and analysis.

As Gorsuch (1983) noted, "whereas the former [EFA] simply finds those factors that best reproduce the variables under the maximum likelihood conditions, the latter [CFA] tests specific hypothesis regarding the nature of the factors." In sum, we used CFA to evaluate the tools of measurements with respect to their sufficiency in fulfilling the criteria of reliability, unidimensionality and validity. The pertinent structures are shown in Table 4.12, and as we can see, the resulting factors are consistent with those of Korgaonkar et al. (1986). Summated scales were computed for each factor.

In order to assess the factors related to industrial print ad campaigns, three separate regression analyses were done, one for each possible outcome of the campaign, i.e., increasing sales, creating a positive attitude and creating awareness. Each one of these outcomes served the role of the dependent variable of the analysis, while the factors emerged in our study were the independent variables of the model.

Table 4.12 Operationalization of the independent variables of the study

Independent variables	Statements	Reliability coefficient alpha
Product uniqueness	The advertised product had unique features for customers	0.838
	The advertised product was superior to competing product(s)	
	The advertised product was highly innovative	
	The advertised product had higher quality than competitors' product(s)	
Competition	The product was launched in a highly competitive market	0.829
	Customers were satisfied with competitors' products	
	The competitors spent a lot of money advertising their product	
	The market was characterized by many competitors	
Agency and client relationships	During the print ad campaign, there were changes in the company's key personnel involved in the campaign	0.893
	During the print ad campaign, there were changes in the agency's key personnel involved in the campaign	
	During the print ad campaign, there were company/client personality conflicts	
Market research	Before advertising, the product customers' needs were carefully studied	0.933
	The communication used in the advertisement was selected on the basis of pretest studies	
	Before advertising, the product test-market studies were undertaken	
	Before launching the print ad campaign, the preliminary market assessments were undertaken	
	The print ad campaign had necessary market research resources	
Resources	The company's personnel involved in the campaign had needed managerial skills	0.925
	The print ad campaign was backed with adequate financial resources	
	The advertiser had adequate advertising skills	
	The print ad campaign was compatible with the advertiser's sales force/distribution policies	

(continued)

Table 4.12 (continued)

Independent variables	Statements	Reliability coefficient alpha
Media selection	The product was advertised in the right print media at the right time and place	0.943
	The characteristics of the print media audience were congruent with the characteristics of the customers	
	The selection of print media was based on careful analysis of demand factors	
	The product was advertised in the appropriate print media	
	The selection of print media was based mainly on cost consideration (reverse item)	
Message and creativity	The communication used in the advertisement highlighted the uniqueness of the product	0.966
	The communication used in the advertisement differentiated the advertised product from the competitors' product	
	The print ad campaign had the support of talented creative staff	
	The headline/slogan used in the campaign was compatible with overall advertising objectives	
	The communication used in the advertisement was felt to be persuasive	
	The creative staff was successful in translating its ideas into a unique print ad campaign	
	The communication used in the advertisement was well targeted	
	The copy platform was felt to be unique and creative	

Increasing Sales

The results of this multiple regression analysis are shown in Table 4.13. These results indicate that the regression model is significant at 0.01 level. Moreover, the model suggests that the factors which are correlated with increasing sales are agency and client relationship and media selection. If the goal of the print ad campaign is to increase sales, it is important for

Table 4.13 Multiple regression results (Dependent variable: Sales)

Variable	Standardized Beta	t statistics
Product uniqueness	0.111	1.283
Competition	0.146	1.568
Agency and client relationships	−0.385	−3.868[a]
Market research	0.098	1.091
Resources	0.141	1.559
Media selection	0.256	2.651[a]
Message and creativity	0.159	1.673

[a]Significant at 0.05 level or better
$R^2 = 0.20$
Durbin-Watson $= 1.667$
$F = 14.519$

Table 4.14 Multiple regression results (Dependent variable: Attitude)

Variable	Standardized Beta	t statistics
Product uniqueness	0.038	0.667
Competition	0.041	0.681
Agency and client relationships	−0.248	−4.075[a]
Market research	0.290	4.823[a]
Resources	0.332	5.071[a]
Media selection	0.311	4.287[a]
Message and creativity	0.251	4.138[a]

[a]Significant at 0.01 level
$R^2 = 0.67$
Durbin-Watson $= 1.962$
$F = 38.551$

the company to maintain a smooth working relationship with its agency and be able to select the right print media.

Creating Favorable Attitude

The results of the regression analysis shown in Table 4.14 indicate that media selection, resources invested in the campaign, market research support, creativity of the message and agency–client relationship were significantly related to creating favorable attitude toward the advertised product. These findings suggest that in order to create a favorable attitude toward the advertised product, the company should carefully select the media to advertise the product. Moreover, the probability of achieving this communication goal increases to the extent to which there are sufficient resources for the campaign together with a smooth working relationship between the company and the agency staff. The selection of a persuasive and creative message, supported by adequate market research efforts, is also significantly important in achieving favorable attitude toward the advertised product.

Creating Awareness

The results (Table 4.15) indicate that the four factors which are significantly correlated with the communication goal of creating awareness are agency–company relationship, message creativity, resources of the campaign and market research. The results suggest that if the communication goal of the print ad campaign is to generate awareness, it is important for the company to have a smooth relationship with the advertising agency. In addition, it can be inferred that a creative message together with adequate campaign resources and market research support can increase the possibility of achieving this goal.

For many years, the importance of advertising has been recognized in the business world, making, thus, advertising campaign strategies

Table 4.15 Multiple regression results (Dependent variable: Awareness)

Variable	Standardized Beta	t statistics
Product uniqueness	−0.018	−0.361
Competition	−0.071	−1.472
Agency and client relationships	−0.314	−5.861[a]
Market research	0.283	4.935[a]
Resources	0.422	7.482[a]
Media selection	0.086	1.639
Message and creativity	0.517	9.667[a]

[a]Significant at 0.01 level
$R^2 = 0.73$
Durbin-Watson $= 2.008$
$F = 70.272$

essential for every business (Vâlcean 2011). Advertising surrounds individuals and businesses and companies spend billions on advertising in the hope to influence their desire to purchase products or services; in the meantime, they expect to see an increase in their profits, while they do not always have the adequate know-how. The results of the study lead us to some very interesting and important conclusions that may be useful to the industrial marketing executives with regard to the antecedents of successful ad campaigns.

First of all, it is true that the outcome of an industrial print ad campaign is correlated with certain factors similar to those that Korgaonkar et al. (1986) found for industrial advertising campaigns in general. The way these factors influence the outcome of a print ad campaign-changes with respect to the intended objective of the campaign. Thus, the factors which are related to campaign success are dependent on the intended outcome, i.e., sales/attitude/awareness. Consequently, the definition of the communication goals of an industrial print ad campaign prior to the campaign is of major importance, in order for the managers to be able to pay special attention to the factors that are mostly going to affect the outcome of the campaign.

Moreover, the relationship between the company and the advertising agency seems to be a very crucial factor regardless of the communication goal. This means that the company has to maintain a smooth working relationship with the agency in order to increase the probability of success for the campaign. This also underlines the dominant role of advertising agencies in the industrial market, which is partly explained by the lack of promotional experience of industrial companies.

When the goal of the print ad campaign is to increase awareness or create favorable attitude, it is important for the company to have a creative message together with adequate campaign resources and market research support, in order to create a successful campaign. For those companies that aim to achieve sales increase and favorable attitude for their products, the need for a careful selection of media is also apparent. As far as the awareness goal is concerned, a possible explanation for these findings can be sought from the fact that the creative part of the ad has always been considered as the one that primarily promotes the image of a product, a brand or a company.

If we try to shed light on the part concerning the creation of a positive customer attitude, it must be inferred that a prerequisite for this goal is the definite and successful targeting of the correct group of customers. The company can then explore the needs of the target group through market research and decide on the appropriate media to promote the product in such a way that the customers would adopt a positive attitude for it. Moreover, it is of great importance that the company shall lay the promotion of the product on the hands of creative managers who can back the print ad with adequate characteristics in order to have more appeal. The existence of financial resources and the smooth cooperation with the advertising agency can give a great boost to the progress of the aforementioned procedure.

The regression model concerning sales had a relatively low value of R^2 which validates our argument that business advertising does not have a direct impact on sales. As Hutt and Speh argue (2004): "Personal selling, price, product performance and competitive actions have a more direct relationship to sales leads and it is almost impossible to sort out the impact of advertising."

In sum, the findings of this study that investigated industrial print ad campaigns are consistent with the findings of the study of Korgaonkar et al. (1986), which dealt with industrial advertising campaigns in general. Still the need for further research is apparent. Industrial executives and researchers ought to assess the outcome of a campaign from both the company's and the customer's point of view in order to get an integrated perspective of the print ad effectiveness.

Limitations and Suggestions for Future Research

The results of the study are subject to some limitations. First of all, a concern pertains to the use of the specific set of characteristics, since other characteristics are likely to influence print ad effectiveness. Thus, future research should study the impact of other characteristics such as the use of appeals, the size of the illustration, the number of type styles or the space used for text in the ad.

Another limitation of the study concerns the geographical context in which the research was carried out. The ability to draw any conclusions is obviously limited since we cannot easily generalize our findings to all companies or countries. Thus, replication is needed to ensure confidence in the stability of the findings. However, the importance and the validity of our findings is not reduced, to the extent that they increase our knowledge and understanding of the way a print ad can be effective in the industrial market. Future research should be conducted in other countries using a different sampling frame and, thus, improving our knowledge on the specific issue.

Since determining advertising effectiveness is a crucial procedure, more research is needed to uncover the mechanisms concerning the usage of the appropriate effectiveness measure. In addition, industrial executives and researchers ought to assess the effectiveness of an industrial ad from both the company's and the customer's point of view in order to get an integrated perspective of the print ad effectiveness.

References

Assael, H., Kofron, J. H., & Burgi, W. (1967). Advertising Performance as a Function of Print Ad Characteristics. *Journal of Advertising Research*.

Baack, W. D., Wilson, R. T., van Dessel, M. M., & Patti, C. (2015). Advertising to businesses: Does creativity matter? *Industrial Marketing Management, 55,* 169–177.

Baker, W. (2000). An empirical test of an updated relevance-accessibility model of advertising effectiveness. *Journal of Advertising, 30*(1), 1–14.

Bandalos, B. (1996). Confirmatory factor analysis. In J. Stevens (Ed.), *Applied multivariate statistics for the social sciences* (3rd ed., pp. 389–420). Mahwah, NJ: Lawrence Erlbaum.

Bansal, M., & Gupta, S. (2014). Impact of newspaper advertisement on consumer behaviour. *Global Journal of Finance and Management, 6*(7), 669–674.

Belch, G., & Belch, M. (2009). *Advertising and promotion: An integrated marketing communications perspective* (8th ed.). New York: McGraw-Hill/Irwin.

Bendixen, M. (1993). Advertising effects and effectiveness. *European Journal of Marketing, 27*(10), 19–32.

Briggs, R. (2006). Marketers who measure the wrong thing get faulty answers. *Journal of Advertising Research, 46*(4), 462–468.

Cavanaugh, S. (1976). Setting objectives and evaluating the effectiveness of trade show exhibits. *Journal of Advertising Research, 9,* 3–9.

Cengiz, Y., Telci, E. E., Bodur, M., & Iscioglu, T. E. (2011). Source characteristics and advertising effectiveness. *International Journal of Advertising, 30*(5), 889–914.

Chamblee, R., & Sandler, D. (1992). Business-to-business advertising: Which layout style works best? *Journal of Advertising Research, 32,* 39–46.

Chattopadhyay, A., & Laborie, J. (2005). Managing brand experience: The market contact audit. *Journal of Advertising Research, 45*(1), 9–16.

Craik, F. I., & Lockhart, R. S. (1972). Levels of processing: A framework for memory research. *Journal of Verbal Learning and Verbal Behavior, 11*(6), 671–684.

Cretu, A., & Brodie, R. (2007). The influence of brand image and company reputation where manufacturers market to small firms: A customer value perspective. *Industrial Marketing Management, 36*(2), 230–240.

Diamond, D. S. (1968). A quantitative approach to magazine advertisements format selection. *Journal of Marketing Research, 5,* 376–386.

Donovan, A. (1979). Awareness of trade-press advertising. *Journal of Advertising Research, 19,* 33–35.

Estévez, M., & Fabrizio, D. (2014). Advertising effectiveness: An approach based on what consumers perceive and what advertisers need. *Open Journal of Business and Management, 2,* 180–188.

Feld, S., Frenzen, H., Krafft, M., Peters, K., & Verhoef, P. C. (2012). The effects of mailing design characteristics on direct mail campaign performance. *International Journal of Research in Marketing, 30*(2), 143–159.

Finn, A. (1988). Print ad recognition readership scores: An information processing perspective. *Journal of Marketing Research, 25*(2), 168–177.

Fletcher, A. D., & Zeigler, S. K. (1978). Creative strategy and magazine ad readership. *Journal of Advertising Research, 18*(1), 29–33.

Frankel, L. R., & Solov, B. M. (1963). Does recall of an advertisement depend on its position in the magazine? *Journal of Advertising Research, 2,* 28–32.

Gorsuch, R. L. (1983). *Factor analysis* (2nd ed.). Hillsdale, NJ: Lawrence Erlbaum.

Greyser, S. A. (1978). Academic research managers can use. *Journal of Advertising Research, 18,* 9–14.

Hanssens, D., & Weitz, B. A. (1980). The effectiveness of industrial print advertisements across product categories. *Journal of Marketing Research, 27,* 294–306.

Havens, G. N. (1980, April 4). Industrial advertising grows in scope, status, and strategic value. *Marketing News.*

Henson, R. K., & Roberts, J. K. (2006). Use of exploratory factor analysis in published research. *Educational and Psychological Measurement, 66,* 393–416.

Herzog, R. E. (1985). How design engineers activity affects supplies. *Business Marketing, 70,* 143.

Holbrook, M. B., & Lehmann, D. R. (1980). Form versus content in predicting starch scores. *Journal of Advertising Research.*

Hutt, M. D., & Speh, T. W. (2004). *Business marketing management—A strategic view of industrial and organizational markets* (8th ed.). Mason, OH: Thomson South-Western.

Jensen, M. B., & Jepsen, A. L. (2007). Low attention advertising processing in B2B markets. *Journal of Business & Industrial Marketing, 4*(5), 342–348.

Kamp, E., & MacInnis, D. J. (1995). Characteristics of portrayed emotions in commercials: When does what is shown in ads affect viewers? *Journal of Advertising Research, 35*(6), 19–29.

Keshari, P., Asha, J., & Sangeeta, J. (2013). Constituents of advertising effectiveness: A study of select service advertising. *Journal of Services Research, 12*(2), 111–127.

Korgaonkar, P. K., Bellenger, D. N., & Smith, A. E. (1986). Successful industrial advertising campaigns. *Industrial Marketing Management, 15,* 123–128.

LaPlaca, P. J. (2013). Research priorities for B2B marketing research. *Revista Española de Investigación de Marketing, 17*(2), 135–150.

Lavidge, R. J., & Steiner, G. A. (1961). A model for predictive measurements of advertising effectiveness. *Journal of Marketing, 25,* 59–62.

Leigh, J., Zinkhan, G., & Swaminahan, V. (2006). Dimensional relationships of recall and recognition measures with selected cognitive and affective aspects of print ads. *Journal of Advertising, 35*(1), 105–122.

Ljungren, R. G. (1976). Building more business with industrial direct mail advertising. *Industrial Marketing Management, 10,* 277–281.

Lohtia, R., Johnston, W. J., & Aab, L. (1995). Business-to-business advertising: What are the dimensions of an effective print ad? *Industrial Marketing Management, 24*(5), 369–378.

Lynch, J., & de Chernatony, L. (2004). The power of emotion: Brand communication in business-to-business markets. *The Journal of Brand Management, 11*(5), 403–419.

Maheshwari, P., Seth, N., & Gupta, A. K. (2014). Advertisement effectiveness: A review and research agenda. *International Journal of Social, Behavioral, Educational, Economic, Business and Industrial Engineering, 8*(12), 3903–3907.

McBride, B. (2007). *Measuring print advertising.* Retrieved from http://www.marketingpower.com/content1292.php.

McQuarrie, E., & Phillips, B. (2005). Indirect persuasion in advertising: How consumers process metaphors presented in pictures and words. *Journal of Advertising, 34*(2), 7–20.

Morrill, J. E. (1970). Industrial advertising pays off. *Harvard Business Review, 48*, 4–14.

Mudambi, S. (2002). Branding importance in business-to-business markets: Three buyer clusters. *Industrial Marketing Management, 31*(6), 525–533.

Mudambi, S., Doyleb, P., & Wong, V. (1997). An exploration of branding in industrial markets. *Industrial Marketing Management, 26*(5), 433–446.

Nayak, K., & Shah, B. (2015). Effectiveness of newspaper print ads. *Indian Journal of Applied Research, 5*(2), 328–331.

Novak-Marcincin, J., Modrak, V., & Okwiet, K. B. (2012). Advertising and its importance in management on the example of SME's enterprise X. *RevistaRomână de Statistică – Supliment Trim, IV*, 201–208.

Olsen, G. D., Pracejus, J., & O'guinn, T. (2012). Print advertising: White space. *Journal of Business Research, 65*(6), 855–860.

Parasuraman, A. (1981). The relative importance of industrial promotion tools. *Industrial Marketing Management, 10*, 277–281.

Pieters, R., Wedel, M., & Zhang, J. (2007). Optimal feature advertising design under competitive clutter. *Management Science, 53*(11), 1815–1828.

Printhvi, B. J., & Dash, M. (2013). Comparative effectiveness of radio, print and web advertising. *Asia Pacific Journal of Marketing & Management Review, 2*(7), 12–19.

Saunders, J., & Watt, F. (1979). Do brand names differentiate identical industrial products? *Industrial Marketing Management, 8*(2), 114–123.

Shimp, T. 2007. *Integrated marketing promotions in advertising and promotion*(7th ed.). Mason, OH: Thompson South-Western.

Silk, A. J., & Geiger, F. P. (1972). Advertisement size and the relationship between product usage and advertising exposure. *Journal of Marketing Research*, 22–26.

Shipley, D., & Howard, P. (1993). Brand-naming industrial products. *Industrial Marketing Management, 22*(1), 59–66.

Sinha, A. P., Agarwal, N., & Johnson. (2012). B2B advertising in an emerging economy: Rational vs. emotional appeals, and gender stereotypes. *Social Science Research Network*. (Indian institute of Technology).

Smith, R. E., & Swinyard, W. R. (1982). Information response models: An integrated approach. *Journal of Marketing, 46,* 81–93.

Soley, L. C. (1986). Copy length and industrial advertising readership. *Industrial Marketing Management, 15*(3), 245–251.

Soley, L., & Reid, L. (1983a). Industrial ad readership as a function of headline type. *Journal of Advertising, 12*(1), 34–38.

Soley, L., & Reid, L. (1983b). Predicting industrial ad readership. *Industrial Marketing Management, 12,* 201–206.

Stapel, J. (1998). Recall and recognition: A very close relationship. *Journal of Advertising Research, 38*(4), 41–45.

Terkan, R. (2014). Importance of creative advertising and marketing according to university students' perspective. *International Review of Management and Marketing, 4*(3), 239–246.

Toncar, M., & Munch J. (2001). Consumer response to tropes in print advertising, *Journal of Advertising, 30*(1), 55–65.

Troldahl, V. C., & Jones, R. L. (1965). Predictors of newspaper advertisement readership. *Journal of Advertising Research.*

Vâlceanu, G. (2011). A successful advertising campaign. *Holistic Marketing Management, 1*(1), 97–108.

Wason, A., Wright, O., & Dada, L. (2014). Franchising rhetoric: A cross cultural study of B2B advertising. *Australian and New Zealand Marketing Academy (ANZMAC) Conference*, Australia.

Wells, W. (2000). Recognition, recall, and rating sales. *Journal of Advertising Research, 40*(6), 14–20.

Williams, J. D. (1983). Industrial publicity: One of the promotional tools. *Industrial Marketing Management, 12,* 207–211.

Wimmer, R., & Dominick, J. (2006). *Mass media research* (8th ed.). Belmont, CA: Thomson Wadsworth.

Yamanaka, J. (1962). The prediction of ad readership scores. *Journal of Advertising Research, 2,* 18–23.

Yoon, E., & Kijewski, V. (1995). The brand awareness-to-preference link in business markets: A study of the semiconductor manufacturing industry. *Journal of Business-to-Business Marketing, 2*(4), 7–36.

Zinkhan, G. M. (1984). Rating industrial advertisements. *Industrial Marketing Management, 13*(1), 43–48.

5

Achieving Advertising Effectiveness Through Innovation

Abstract This chapter appraises the importance of innovation for business-to-business promotion. The authors state that the survival of organizations today largely lies on their behavior toward innovation, which can lead to a competitive advantage. Similarly, their ability to incorporate innovation into their marketing function is critical and in a way determines the success of many organizations. The authors suggest that regardless of the nature of the marketing communications mix, and irrespective of whether the promotion is traditional or digital or both, innovative communication techniques are always appealing to customers. Is that the case for industrial buyers as well? The future is, by all means, digital, but can we get the benefits of innovation without actually adopting the underlying technologies?

Keywords Innovation · New technologies in Advertising · Innovative B2B communications techniques

What Is Innovation?

The survival of organizations today largely lies on their behavior toward innovation (Tödtling et al. 2009). Innovation, if carefully implemented,

© The Author(s) 2017   **69**
I. Rizomyliotis et al., *Business-to-Business Marketing Communications*,
DOI 10.1007/978-3-319-58783-7_5

can lead to improved productivity and provide the basis for a competitive advantage (Knani 2013), while at the same time, according to Tushman and O'Reilly (2006), the success of many contemporary organizations depends on their ability to incorporate innovation into their culture. Similarly, high-leveled investments are made on research and development and the use of sophisticated systems in various fields of traditional economy. The transition of the global society to the postindustrial stages deeply affects current trends of the world development. Human civilization entered a new stage of evolution—the information society, which is based on the activity constituted by the production processes, distribution and the use of information. At present, in addition to the traditional advertising techniques used to attract the end user, numerous innovative methods get extensively applied. They have emerged recently but are widely adopted by in B2B sphere and receive a broad approval by the target audience. The future is, by all means, digital, but can we get the benefits of innovation without actually adopting the underlying technologies?

Austrian economist Joseph Schumpeter is considered to be the founder of the innovation theory. His approach to this phenomenon and its nature is considered to be classical. According to Mendelova and Zauskova (2015), Schumpeter states that innovations are technologically new or advanced engineering procedures or methods used in practical activities (Mendelova and Zauskova 2015, p. 40). Innovations constitute the result of investment in development and receipt of a new knowledge not applied earlier.

Innovation is a complex developing process of creation, distribution and use of a new idea, which promotes an increase in the overall performance of an organization. At the same time, innovation is not merely an object or approach implemented into the production process but is being successfully implemented as a result of the conducted scientific research or discovery, qualitatively differing from the prior analogues (Maheshwari et al. 2014, p. 3904). In other words, it is a new, nonstandard and original approach or method aimed at providing a solution to the existing problem, which, in the case of the smallest efforts and financial costs, allows achieving desirable results.

Innovation, if carefully implemented in the B2B sector, can lead to improved productivity and provide a basis for the acquisition of a competitive advantage. It is often more valuable in comparison with the traditional resources of business (finance, equipment, labor power), which is particularly evident at the development stage of a new business. It should be noted that in the post-industrial society, the main competitive potential is based on the intellectual equity of the personnel. Moreover, a constant innovative activity is directed at the enhancement of the competitive advantage of goods and services with the main aim of ensuring a steady competitive advantage of the company. Thus, the recent tendency represents a growing rate of investment into the non-traditional creative businesses—the ideas allowing companies to obtain a competitive edge (Srinivasan et al. 2009, p. 24). The innovative type of the competitive behavior differs from the traditional one and is based on the modern representations of the economic science.

At the same time, according to Tushman et al. (2006), the success of many contemporary organizations in B2B sector depends on their ability to incorporate innovation into their culture and communication. This incorporation is represented by the innovative corporate culture, which is a system of the regulations and values adopted by the company and providing a high level of perception, initiation and implementation of innovations. The innovative organization continually enhances its structure, as well as supports and develops the informal structures founded on the sociocultural values, oriented at the creativity and innovations. In other words, such an organization "grows up" the innovative teams, cares for their integration into the company and helps the young employees to receive the resources for the initiation of the new projects (Tushman et al. 2006). In addition, such organizations liquidate obsolete projects, even those headed by the authoritative specialists. The formation and development of the innovative organizations represent the natural sociocultural process, measured by the generations of entrepreneurs.

Innovative activities cover all the creative processes—from the emergence of an idea and up to the production of goods and their promotion, as well as the transformation of the results and development or other scientific and technical achievements in the market (Tushman et al. 2006). Thus, innovation can also be termed as the innovative product or the product of innovative activities. This process is an organized system of consistently performed types of productive activities, and in B2B, it includes several stages, namely the emergence of the innovative idea; the development of the "portfolio of ideas"; conduction of the scientific research aimed at testing the ideas; the selection of the projects for the production; and the creation of the innovative design, as well as the distribution of the mass production in the market (Anan'eva 2013, p. 343). Thus, the whole course of the innovative process should be traced and corrected on the basis of the information about the state of the market of innovations.

The speed of the diffusion of innovation also depends on the efficiency of technological innovation. The process of the distribution of new technologies, also called "diffusion of technologies", acts as an auxiliary element for their use in production and further realization of innovations in the B2B sector. In general, the earlier the company starts the innovative activity, the quicker and cheaper it will be to catch up with the leaders in the market. While the adoption of the related technological advancements can lead to an increase in the competitiveness and the maintenance of a high profitability level, there are various difficulties deriving from both risk aversion and innovation adoption rates (Herault 2013, p. 50; Estevez and Fabrizio 2014, p. 241). Therefore, the attitude toward innovation plays a significant role in its timely adoption. The successful use of innovativeness in practice, according to Herault (2013), relies on the early implementation of the underlying innovative technologies; this allows companies to receive all benefits associated with this activity, so entities should start to conduct technological innovation development as soon as possible.

Innovation and B2B Communication

The innovative advertising technologies are more fascinating, easily acquired and efficient in comparison with those being traditionally applied in the B2B sector. According to the estimates of specialists, their use can increase the sales volume of the represented products by 20–45% (Srinivasan et al. 2009). Large sales volumes and the growth of sales leads to the rise in advertising rates in the B2B sector; accordingly, the need for the development of original and unique methods of advertising is evident. Thus, the constant development of trade is a driving link for advertising; it forces marketing communication managers to search for innovative ways to increase promotion efficiency. Recent research, on the other hand, shows that customers are not satisfied with the standard, conventional types of advertising anymore (Anan'eva 2013). As a result, the customer exposure to advertising decreases and the time of contact with the brand is reduced, and this leads to an increase in the advertising cost per exposure. Apart from that, to achieve maximum effect at such a speed of advertising technologies development, every advertising specialist should stay updated on all occurring events, shifts or transformations in the world of business and be flexible and adaptable to the changing conditions; in other words, be able to make correct decisions. It is possible to determine the most effective approach when offering goods and services to the end user in the B2B context; however, a constant market research work has to be carried out (Maheshwari et al. 2014). The emergence of online research and promotional techniques led to the increase in the number of customers and expanded the circle of the activities even for small companies that initially suffered losses having failed to adapt quickly to the new changes. Innovations in promotion not necessarily linked with new technologies have helped toward this direction and were reported to be rather effective:

> The relationship between innovation and effectiveness should inherently be a basic principle of communication. Advertising has the greatest ability to become effective when the recipient notices the advertising. Innovation is therefore a major prerequisite related to ensuring that advertising campaigns are effective. Such innovation must be thoroughly connected to the other elements of the campaign, including sales and the product itself. (Mendelova and Zauskova 2015, p. 47)

The emergence of innovation in the B2B sector, which positively affects the marketing communication stream, as a rule, leads to the increase in customer demand for particular goods and, thus, an increase in the entity's profits. Accordingly, it becomes the cause of the decline of the profits for rival companies (Srinivasan et al. 2009). In this case, the inability of the other firms to orient quickly under the circumstances and offer something new or earlier unseen by the end users makes most of them to financially collapse.

The new innovative techniques of B2B promotion involuntarily distract consumers conveying, thus, the necessary message of the advertising campaign. In principle, the process of the advertising strategy design requires the formulation of the key characteristics in such a way that they eventually supplement each other. The innovative technologies in the B2B sector allow not only to draw attention to the message but also to make it more appealing to the message receivers, involving them into the advertising plot (Herault 2013). This is true simply because new technologies in communication offer the ability of both customization and interaction. Thus, the innovative activity both in the sphere of promotion and in the overall company's operations constitutes the basis for the entity's survival in the modern market under the conditions of harsh competition.

While the new media advertising is effective, the promotion that entails conceptual innovation can be the most successful channels of communication, for the businesses operating in the B2B sector. However, the good results this can give will maximize with the appropriate selection of the communication platforms. In addition, the application of low-cost and non-conventional advertising methods, such as "guerrilla marketing," can also be treated as innovative promotion that is suitable for the small- and medium-sized B2B business models (Nufer 2013, p. 2; Ay et al. 2010, p. 280). The guerrilla marketing communication strategy assumes the use of the low-budget but effective advertising methods (Hutter and Hoffmann 2011). The term "guerrilla marketing" was introduced by the American marketing specialist Jay Konrad Levinson, who articulated the techniques represented by the unusual outdoor advertising (Wanner 2011; Hutter and Hoffmann 2011). This type of marketing communication strategy can be an enormously effective tool, which allows B2B companies to move on with a low budget and eventually stand out in conditions of fierce and steadily growing competition.

However, the development of a "smart" marketing communication strategy is not enough for the efficient promotion of goods and services in B2B sector. The design of a message that contains originality, appealing to the needs of people is also required (Wanner 2011). Considering the customer, guerrilla advertising is not just an offer to pay attention to the advertised product, but also a real communication, involving a person and not an entire business and can surprise and increase mood. On the contrary, traditional advertisements that are directed to B2B customers can cause the inverted effect; they may seem appropriately designed to meet a business customer but they alienate the individuals. In all, the ability to develop effective promotion methods, even when they extraordinary, is considered a critical asset in the struggle to stimulate sales in the B2B sector (Nufer 2013, p. 3; Ay et al. 2010, p. 283). Fresh and innovative ideas represent the principal investment as to what regards this marketing communication approach. The organizations that quickly and efficiently create and use fresh ideas gain the long-term competitive advantage (Tellis 2009).

In plain words, the challenge is to make all used techniques and material meaningful. In order to effectuate this, managers need to realize that real innovation derives from listening to customers and unlocking customer trends. Essentially, this means that the starting point for all innovative communication will always be the same: the appropriate use of metrics to perform an accurate market research. In that sense, the pillars of innovation in marketing communication have to do with predicting customer preferences and decoding customer feedback. Market research and predictive models can combine data provided from different sources, in different formats and reveal the hidden secrets of customer behavior.

A Holistic Approach of Innovation in B2B Communication

In conclusion, innovation in its general sense refers to the ongoing changes in the economy, industry, society, trends in behavior of buyers, producers and workers. Similarly, innovations represent an effective way of the competitive struggle as they lead to the creation of new requirements, decrease in the product cost, investment inflow, the formation of the desired reputation, and opening and capturing the new markets including the external ones. Therefore, the market and its requirements should always guide it. The innovative methods of promotion are widely applied in all types of business activities, including B2B communication. Due to the rapid advancement and extensive application of new technologies and so-called mass digitalization, the innovative advertising is based on the use of the technical innovations, latest computer technologies and nonstandard methods of informational transfer. Therefore, the organizations cannot fully benefit from the changes without the actual adoption of the underlying technologies as the future of the innovation is in digital format.

However, innovation is not a term that should be used interchangeably with the advanced technological methods; innovative promotion is another way of saying: break the mold, think and act differently. In that sense, new promotional methods are unlikely to replace the traditional ones at present. Innovation equals receptivity and responsiveness; it means being operational toward the market needs with the use of accurate data. Simply put, businesses need to be able to collect, process, analyze and transform data into meaningful information; information that is getting captured in real time and used instantly to communicate with existing customers and prospects. In a way, innovation in marketing communication is an alternative way of saying flexibility to deliver timely and appropriately designed value to customers and prospects.

References

Anan'eva, N. (2013). Advertising activities in innovation economy. *Middle-East Journal of Scientific Research, 16*(3), 342–347.

Ay, C., Aytekin, P., & Nardali, S. (2010). Guerrilla marketing communication tools and ethical problems in guerilla advertising. *American Journal of Economics and Business Administration, 2*(3), 280–286.

Estevez, M., & Fabrizio, D. (2014). Advertising effectiveness: An approach based on what consumers perceive and what advertisers need. *Open Journal of Business and Management, 2,* 180–188.

Herault, S. (2013). Investigating innovations in information systems: How to evaluate the m-advertising effectiveness? *Problems and Perspectives in Management, 11*(2), 48–56.

Hutter, K., & Hoffmann, S. (2011). Guerilla marketing: The nature of the concept and propositions for further research. *Asian Journal of Marketing, 5* 1–16.

Knani, M. (2013). Exploratory study of the impacts of new technology implementation on burnout and presenteeism. *International Journal of Business and Management, 8*(22), 92.

Maheshwari, P., Seth, N., & Gupta, A. (2014). Advertisement effectiveness: A review and research agenda. *International Scholarly and Scientific Research & Innovation, 8*(12), 3903–3907.

Mendelova, D., & Zauskova, A. (2015). Innovation in the Slovak advertising environment. *Communication Today, 6*(1), 38–57.

Nufer, G. (2013). Guerrilla marketing—Innovative or parasitic marketing? *Modern Economy, 4,* 1–6.

Srinivasan, S., Pauwels, K., Silva-Risso, J., & Hanssens, D. (2009). Product innovations, advertising, and stock returns. *Journal of Marketing, 73*(1), 24–43.

Tellis, G. (2009). Generalizations about advertising effectiveness in markets. *Journal of Advertising Research, 49*(2), 240–245.

Tödtling, F., Lehner, P., & Kaufmann, A. (2009). Do different types of innovation rely on specific kinds of knowledge interactions?. *Technovation, 29*(1), 59–71.

Tushman, M., Smith, W., Wood, C. W., Westerman, G., & O'Reilly, C. (2006). *Organizational Designs and Innovation Streams.* Retrieved from http://www.immagic.com/eLibrary/ARCHIVES/GENERAL/HARVARD/H060908T.pdf.

Wanner, M. (2011). More than the consumer eye can see: Guerrilla advertising from an agency standpoint. *The Elon Journal of Undergraduate Research in Communications, 2*(1), 103–109.

6

What Is Next for Business-to-Business Marketing Communication?

Abstract This chapter aims to review the current B2B landscape in terms of the upcoming developments in marketing communications. Industrial marketing managers operate against a background of financial uncertainty and, thus, are in seek for more sophisticated measures of accountability. Recession had a severe impact on advertising budgets given that advertising is still regarded as a cost rather than an investment by manufacturers. At the same time, digitalization brought fundamental changes to the way B2B marketing communication and advertisingare developed, planned and performed. In simple terms, a great digital challenge was posed for B2B firms, against a major financial problem. The authors also provide some implications for B2B marketing managers in the foreseeable future.

Keywords Future of B2B Promotion · Trends in B2B · Advances in B2B Marketing Communication

© The Author(s) 2017
I. Rizomyliotis et al., *Business-to-Business Marketing Communications*,
DOI 10.1007/978-3-319-58783-7_6

Digitalization in B2B Marketing Communication

Businesses-to-business communication and industrial advertising have undergone remarkable transformations in the recent times as businesses are realigning themselves to remain relevant in an ever-changing market. Consumer trends are fast shaping the B2B advertising scene with the rise in the use of social media, visual Web and even with the use of tailored mobile phone applications in improving customer relations; all these have influenced a great deal in restructuring B2B communication and advertising. The digital platforms have propelled B2B advertising to greater heights owing to the constant innovations and refurbishments in the digital world, hence offering multiple avenues to deliver the desired messages to the intended business targets. Therefore, the breakthrough of B2B communication and advertising lies in the way a business will exploit digitalization to gain competitive advantage. While digitalization sometimes comes with various challenges such as the manipulation of large sets of data, companies must remain vigilant as they can now reach a wider audience in addition to several other benefits that traditional media cannot offer.

Businesses-to-business marketing communication has gone through numerous changes over the years in a bid to increase the efficiency and effectiveness in conveying accurate information to the intended target. Many businesses used to promote themselves to prospects through the traditional media such as trade magazines, or even yellow pages ads and brochures, and they have subsequently faced the necessity of altering the way they communicated with their audiences in order to deliver the desired results. The constant innovations and continuous improvements in the technology world have ushered in a new era of doing business that is faster, is cost-effective, and reaches to a wider audience, thus forcing businesses to gradually incorporate various digital tools to enhance their marketing communication performance (Spotts and Weinberger 2010).

Digitalization in B2B marketing communications and advertising is strongly influenced by the consumer trends in the market. With the Internet being easily accessible and the increased use of smartphones, the majority of the target market spend their time in online searching and consuming media, hence prompting businesses to restructure their communication strategy to tap and capture the bigger audience in the digital space. Therefore, businesses are increasingly re-aligning themselves toward the latest market trends to an extent that they will prefer to deal with another business online or using other digital tools as opposed to using the traditional ways (Katona and Sarvary 2014). The use of emails, webinars, blogs and social media such as Facebook, LinkedIn and Twitter have gained popularity in conducting day-to-day communication between two or more businesses due to their accessibility, ease of use and convenience. Similarly, there has been a notable increase in the number of young people now in charge of business organizations and that has had a major influence on the way many businesses use digital tools in conducting their B2B communications. Many young managers prefer digital content and gadgets in most of their day-to-day activities; hence, this directly touches on business-to-business managers' inclination to use digital platforms to perform their communication as well.

Emerging Advances in B2B Marketing Communication

The Internet is surely one of the factors that have accelerated the revolution of the digitalization era, thus offering business opportunities not only in reducing costs and providing easy access to the market, but also in establishing a platform for the business to interact with its prospects and gather information about their purchasing patterns. B2B companies can gather information about their prospective business targets within the shortest time possible, enabling them to make customized messages focusing on the needs of their prospects and delivering messages directly to their prospects in record time. Still, businesses need to bear in mind that contemporary business customers are well-informed and sophisticated and they relentlessly use various tools to gather information about the products they want. At the same time, they are fully aware of the marketing tricks managers use to guide their decision-making; thus, it is the duty of B2B managers to ensure that their online communications are reliable, sincere and clear to eliminate any doubt or suspicions (Jap and Reibstein 2010). Business-to-business promotion in the modern day relies more and more on building and maintaining great relationships with clients, and therefore, companies must take the time to study their prospects' activities online and be keen to establishing honest and lasting relationships with them.

Social Media

Many businesses are establishing their social identities online on social media platforms such as Facebook, YouTube, LinkedIn, Twitter, Instagram, WhatsApp and many more social media platforms as they target to interact and build tight relationships with their targets. According to Giakoumaki et al. (2016), B2B communication and advertising tend to be more effective when using LinkedIn and Twitter due to the professional outlook that they portray. LinkedIn provides a company with a platform to share their content or events, while a Facebook and Twitter offer platforms for discussions about a company's products, thus being able to not only communicate a business' products to another business but also gather substantial information from the feedbacks and discussions about the product in real time. B2B social media communication and advertising messages must always be brief, clear and straight to the point to capture the attention of the prospective business clients as many do not spend most their times on social media reading or watching long advertisements. It is, therefore, important for B2B social media communication to prioritize on its content and put in measures and strategies to run and maintain the social media accounts effectively.

Mobile Advertising

Mobile phones are hailed as the biggest transformers of digital marketing due to their rapid evolution and innovations and accessibility by close to over 80% of the market. Most of the companies are using mobile phones for their day-to-day activities, hence enabling companies to successfully deliver B2B advertising messages to their prospective clients with ease. B2B messages can be conveyed via different channels including short text messages, direct calls, mobile applications, Internet emails and messaging and many others. Over 60% of B2B businesses have mobile applications and sites, thus facilitating smooth relay of B2B communication and messages to the intended customers (Freundt et al. 2013). The lion's share of social media communications, emails and search information are carried out using mobile phones; hence, B2B companies must dedicate themselves in developing their mobile platforms to effectively convey their advertising messages.

Content Marketing

Content marketing is also a digital B2B communication tool to be used in the future. It is already used by companies in order to create online material and shared it using digital platforms such as blogs and videos. Their intentions are not to explicitly promote a brand but to avail information about the brand with the intention of triggering interests in their products. According to the research, there is a high demand for content marketing as depicted by several research studies, which show that the demand for content went up by 20% in Q4 of 2015 (DeMers 2016). Being one of the mostly used digital tools by B2B companies for their marketing communications, content marketing is quickly evolving as customers prefer short captivating messages that yet provide all the information needed about a particular product (La et al. 2009). B2B customers usually require substantial information about a specific product they are looking for, hence advertising messages based on content marketing usually come in handy in conveying all the information that customers are seeking. Therefore, B2B marketing communication managers should mainly direct their efforts to convey relevant information required to arouse interest and form positive attitudes toward the product.

Email Marketing

Email marketing is considered to be one of the least costly digital tools for B2B communication and advertising that aids in generating and driving leads, and building and enhancing business relationships.

A professionally crafted B2B advertising message via email is capable of not only generating a sale but also triggering a sale and enhances a business relationship (Biemans et al. 2010). B2B email marketing can be used to draw attention to other digital media tools of the company such as blogs, social media platforms, company mobile phone contacts and Web sites. A B2B purchasing decision cannot be done by a single person in the company; therefore, the business advertising message through the email should not be sent to only one person but instead should be targeted to several key people in the company who are either the final decision-makers or the influencers. B2B companies must, therefore, organize an email marketing communication strategy in accordance with the overall marketing communication objectives, so that content they can carry out a consistent message delivery.

Channel Integration

B2B organizations handle tens of digital media tools, which if not properly managed will prove to be cumbersome and ineffective to handle. There will be also a tendency of focusing on a few digital channels at the expense of others; thus, without an appropriate selection of digital channels, managers will end up delivering unfruitful and expensive marketing communications. Integration of the digital channels will not only secure for the consistency and effectiveness of all the digital marketing channels, the business employs, but will also ensure the uniformity of all the advertising and business communication messages across all of the digital channels, thus enabling mangers to reach a much wider audience with the same message at the same time (Habibi et al. 2015). B2B channel integration also aids in generating more leads tracking the number of visitors on B2B Web sites and online social sites. In that sense, it is easier for marketing communication managers to contact customers and successfully convey to them a custom-made advertising message. Channel integration in B2B also offers opportunities of re-marketing and re-targeting whereby using Google AdWords, previous B2B advertising messages can be delivered again to former site visitors who had accessed the information via Google's search engine

(Spotts et al. 2014). This option can be available for the longest time possible even up to years with it being replicated on social media platforms such as LinkedIn, Twitter and Facebook where programs have been developed to deliver these services.

B2B Buyers Like Stories Too

The future of B2B marketing communication is going to be more personal as B2B buyers are becoming more self-focused; thus, B2B marketing managers in the future will have to come up with new strategies of generating leads and delivering effective marketing communication messages to the market. Many B2B decision-makers are young people who have come with them new trends and strategies that are more personal as they tend to shape organizations to resemble their character and philosophies, a fact that has trickled down to various business departments including marketing (Samanta 2011). B2B marketing communication managers, having fully embraced the digital marketing strategy, must start creating other strategies that incorporate various aspects of business-to-consumer personalized marketing communication strategies in their bid to reach and attract a wider audience in B2B organizations. B2B communication managers will also play an oversight role that will ensure the proper and smooth management of digital channels. Managers will be responsible to effectively select the appropriate communication channels in their effort to successfully engage different customers and address their concerns and complaints before they escalate into crises.

The great recession of 2008 left many B2B companies to dip in financial crises, thus forcing them to rethink their future advertising channels; the latter would now have to be cost-efficient, reliable and effective. Coupled with the younger generations beginning to occupy positions of decision-making in B2B companies, the great recession and digitalization swayed away a big chunk of advertising business from traditional print media to digital platforms (Freundt et al. 2013). Therefore, B2B marketing communication is going to be largely digitized as B2B companies are starting to avoid the costly print media advertising in favor of digital media as a way of cost cutting without upsetting the effectiveness of their promotion. The future B2B buyers have pledged to access information via digital platforms. As a result, and while B2B buyers are driven by a desire of seeking for information faster and a need of finding solutions faster, the delivery of B2B advertising messages through print media will eventually be further sidelined in favor of digitalization.

Furthermore, since most of the B2B marketing communication managers and B2B buyers are becoming tech savvy, less attention will be placed on print media; hence, they will be least preferred as the best channels to convey advertising media. B2B managers can easily access and use modern tech gadgets such as smart mobile phones and computers, and similarly, all kinds of information including advertising messages are available digitally too. Thus, B2B marketing communication is expected to witness an additional drop in print media in favor of digital media as B2B companies are also seeking cheaper advertising media to communicate their messages to their intended business targets. This drop in media in the future is therefore anticipated on the basis of cost cutting as well as the strong influence of the ever-advancing technology.

B2B buyers are less traditional than they used to be and will certainly resemble consumers in the near future. At least in the way they prefer to receive promotion or have access to information. As mentioned before, the B2B industry is witnessing a takeover by a younger and vibrant generation that pays little attention or totally has no interest in print media. The younger crops of B2B managers want quicker access to a wider range of information that is readily available with much ease. Unlike digital media, searching a wider variety of advertising information on print media is cumbersome, a fact that B2B managers will avoid at any cost (Spotts and Weinberger 2010). Personalized communication and customization have always been a given in B2B markets, and digital tools offer cost-efficient ways to tackle this issue. What is more, due to the rise in the cost of living, as the years go by, it will be even costlier to convey a B2B advert on print media. Unlike digital media, where B2B managers can firmly identify their targets and directly send them their advertising messages and instantly have feedbacks, print media can only offer low response rates and a broader market targeting.

Thus, B2B companies are estimated to opt for quicker, interactive and cheaper marketing communication media, that is, digital media.

Similarly, marketing communication managers' role is changing as well. Even in B2B, a market where things are considered to be more bulky in terms of operations, speed and changing habits, managers will have to be constantly creating new marketing communication messages that are clear, accurate and in any case not excessive. In plain words, effective B2B advertising messages will be the ones that are reduced in length in that there will be increased demand for precise messages that are straight to the point. Accordingly, for this to happen, most of the B2B marketing communication managers will have to include more research in their job description and additional decision-making skills in their role. They are expected to act more like consultants and research analysts and spend most of their time researching and creating timely, tailor-made and relevant content for their existing and prospective clients. With the changing demographic in B2B key decision-making and influential positions, B2B marketing communication managers will be forced to dedicate substantial amounts of time to research appropriate content that will suit their intended business targets (Moore et al. 2015); hence, the recent outburst of digitalization is yet to affect massively all marketing communication functions, in the years to come.

Implications for B2B Managers in the Foreseeable Future

The success of B2B marketing communication and advertising strategies will largely depend on the way the companies further exploit the use of digital platform to gain competitive advantage through communication. Digital disruption has redefined B2B marketing and business communication activities, forcing B2B managers to develop comprehensive digital strategies to take advantage of the digitalization. However, digitalization poses a number of challenges including high costs of digitizing an entire B2B company's departments and business functions and also may lead to a tarnished publicity if the information relayed to the market appears to be inaccurate or misleading. B2B organizations must, therefore, conduct an extensive audit to verify the business functions and ascertain the costs in order to create and manage digital platforms that will deliver the intended results. In all, B2B organizations must endeavor to relay to the market clear information through the most appropriate (traditional not excluded) media in addition to establishing a digital unit that specifically takes care of customers' queries and feedbacks.

At the same time, B2B marketing communication managers need to learn to trust their target audience and allow them to contribute to the creation of content and, in turn, to the creation of value. Value co-creation will give immense power and dynamic to the marketing communication process and will ultimately lead to more meaningful campaigns and long-lasting relationships. Those who refuse to understand that it is no longer acceptable for B2B brands to be overly corporate in tone or even boring will inevitably stay behind. B2B buyer audiences, now more than ever, are eager to assert their right to be listened to; they demand from businesses to go beyond plain data collections and need room to express themselves. They now wish to leave their mark across all stages of the sales cycle to and receive a marketing communication campaign around those insights.

With the intensity that the means of communication are currently changing, managers tend to disregard that the success of all brands will always be a function of knowing the customer. From the arrival of social media, the influx of the mobile communications to just about all kinds of communication, consumer trends and customer behavior remain in the core of the B2B buying process. In an ever-changing business world, customer orientation is a constant that managers need to respect. The only meaningful answer to the rapidly and perhaps overwhelming shifting to the digital era is brand consistency; and that must be a priority when offering customer value. It is the responsibility of B2B marketing communication managers to create a memorable and eminent customer experience by acknowledging that without it, no brand, no matter how important it is, can be viable in the long run.

In other words, B2B brands should be developed on the basis of robust market research and on the grounds of accurately predicted B2B buyers' preferences and needs regardless of the platforms the businesses choose to use. The bottom line is to make communications work intensively toward the same direction even when they are initiated from different areas of the same business. B2B customers expect businesses to be able to deliver high-quality and establish seamless interaction with B2B brands across all existing platforms; consistency in communication is again the answer.

To achieve this consistency, B2B marketing communication managers need to have a holistic approach to the communication initiatives. Starting with an integrated marketing communication culture, marketers should be open-minded and brave enough to readily push boundaries. It is true that new technologies are nearly universally regarded as valuable and difficult to counterfeit; and yes, some of the existing advanced materials have industrial and scientific applications. But what is really scarce, and what finally matters most, is the ability to make a step further from just a sizeable presence on social media; B2B marketers need to be relentless in pursuing unique selling proposition within their marketing communication. They must in a way stop selling products and start communicating stories, bringing more interaction rather than just promotion into their strategy. The business of B2B communications is changing, and it is imperative that marketing communication managers not only keep pace, but also manage to stay one step ahead, not necessarily in terms of technology adoption but essentially in terms of customer orientation and understanding.

References

Biemans, W. G., Makovec, B. M., & Malshe, A. (2010). Marketing-sales interface configurations in B2B firms. *Industrial Marketing Management, 39*(2), 183–194.

DeMers, J. (2016). The top 7 content marketing trends that will dominate 2016. *Forbes.* Retrieved from https://www.forbes.com/sites/jaysondemers/2015/10/01/the-top-7-content-marketing-trends-that-will-dominate-2016/#63f48e751a96.

Freundt, J., Hillenbrand, P., & Lehmann, S. (2013). How B2B companies talk past their customers. *McKinsey Quarterly.* Retrieved from http://www.mckinsey.com/business-functions/marketing-and-sales/our-insights/how-b2b-companies-talk-past-their-customers.

Giakoumaki, C., Avlonitis, G. J., & Baltas, G. (2016). Does ingredient advertising work? Some evidence on its impact. *The Journal of Business & Industrial Marketing, 31*(7), 901–913.

Habibi, F., Hamilton, C. A., Valos, M. J., & Callaghan, M. (2015). E-marketing orientation and social media implementation in B2B marketing. *European Business Review, 27*(6), 638–655.

Jap, S., & Reibstein, D. (2010). Introduction to the special issue on B2B research. *Marketing Letters, 21*(3), 207–209.

Katona, Z., & Sarvary, M. (2014). Maersk line: B2B social media- "It's communication, not marketing". *California Management Review, 56*(3), 142–156.

La, V., Patterson, P., & Styles, C. (2009). Client-perceived performance and value in professional B2B services: An international perspective. *Journal of International Business Studies, 40*(2), 274–300.

Moore, J. N., Raymond, M. A., & Hopkins, C. D. (2015). Social selling: A comparison of social media usage across process stage, markets, and sales job functions. *Journal of Marketing Theory and Practice, 23*(1), 1–20.

Samanta, I. (2011). Factors influence B2B relationships in medium-sized firms: Traditional vs. e-commerce. *Journal of Marketing and Operations Management Research, 1*(1), 37–63.

Spotts, H. E., & Weinberger, M. G. (2010). Marketplace footprints: Connecting marketing communication and corporate brands. *European Journal of Marketing, 44*(5), 591–609.

Spotts, H. E., Weinberger, M. G., & Weinberger, M. F. (2014). Publicity and advertising: What matter most for sales? *European Journal of Marketing, 48*(11), 1986–2008.

Index

© The Editor(s) (if applicable) and The Author(s) 2017
I. Rizomyliotis et al., *Business-to-Business Marketing Communications*,
DOI 10.1007/978-3-319-58783-7

91

CPI Antony Rowe
Chippenham, UK
2017-07-18 21:29